TRIAL OF THE CENTURIES

FARAG vs. DEEP STATE

ISLAMIC SHARIA

AND TERROR

THAT DISCLOSED THE

NUCLEAR CRIME

OF THE CENTURY

TAREK FARAG

COPYRIGHT AUGUST 2018
THIRD EDITION

DEDICATION

TO ALL THE VICTIMS OF:
ISLAMIC TERROR AND THEIR FAMILIES;
OUR CORRUPT LEGAL SYSTEM;
THE NEGLIGENCE OF OUR SECURITY AGENCIES; AND
THE MISERABLE FAILURE OF OUR AGENCIES THAT
THEIR JOBS WERE TO PROTECT THE LIVES AND
PROPERTIES OF THE CITIZENS, BUT DID NOT DO
THEIR JOBS WITHOUT ANYONE QUESTIONING THEM.

TO THOSE VICTIMS, THIS BOOK COULD BE A GOOD HELP.

QUOTES

The ratio of good Judges to all judges is comparable to the ratio of good lawyers to all lawyers.

(Tarek Farag)

****

When we have judges on our Supreme Court that openly establish their opinions on their political views, we can realize that our entire legal and justice system are profoundly corrupt.

(Tarek Farag)

****

A wise man told me that in this country, you could get all the justice you can afford.

(Wise Man)

****

Many people swap their goals with their tools and vice versa.

(Tarek Farag)

****

Unfortunately, we have a legal system not a justice system, which demonstrate how the courts made **their goals** to **follow the legal procedures instead of achieving justice**, while they should have made their **goals to achieve justice by following the legal procedures**!

(Tarek Farag)

****

If the truth is harmful to some people, let it be, so that those people can change their positions to avoid harming themselves and others.

(Tarek Farag)

****

My respect to you begins by respecting my self, and ends at how you respect yourself.

As for the ideologies, I am not obligated to respect any, and I do not obligate others to respect my ideology, because its respect comes from its superior teachings not by forcing others to respect it.

(Tarek Farag)

****

But that's always a certain way to recognize a fascist: when he's more powerful he kills everything that's different from him, he uses only brute force while law breaks like glass under his boots. And then, when he loses and when he's weak, he invokes the law and tolerance of differences.

Andrej Nikolaidis

****

TABLE OF CONTENTS

    The Purpose Of This Book
    Introduction To Third Edition
    Introduction
1   The Original Complaint
2   Notice To File Initial Status Report
3   Motion To Enter An Order
4   Order Denying The Motion To Enter An Order
5   Motion To Reconsider And Amend
6   Court Order Denying The Motion To Reconsider And Granting Leave To Amend
7   Amended Complaint
8   Emails Exchanged Between Plaintiff And Government Lawyers
9   Emails Exchanged Between Plaintiff And Government Lawyers
10 Status Report
11 Motion For Protection
12 Order Denying Protection
13 Second Amended Complaint
14 Certification Of Plaintiff
15 Defendants' Motion To Dismiss
16 Memorandum In Support Of Motion To Dismiss Second Amended Complaint
17 Motion For Leave To Respond To Defendants Motion
18 Order Granting Motion For Leave To Respond
19 Motion To Strike Defendants' Motion To Dismiss
20 Order Denying Plaintiff's Motion To Strike Defendants' Motion To Dismiss
21 Plaintiff's Response To Defendant's Motion To Dismiss His Second Amended Complaint

22	The Government's Reply In Support Of Its Motion To Dismiss The Second Amended Complaint
23	Motion To Clarify Plaintiff's Positions In Response To Government's Reply
24	Order Deeming Plaintiff's Motion To Clarify A Surreply
25	Order Re-Setting Status Hearing
26	Order Granting Defendants' Motion To Dismiss
27	Court Order And Opinion
28	Motion To Reconsider The Court Order Dismissing The Complaint
29	Order Denying Plaintiff's Motion To Reconsider
30	The Nuclear Crime Of The Century
31	Letter To Trump Warning Him From The Russia Craze
32	Letter To Trump Warning Him From The Doj
33	Letter To Trump Warning And Informing Him About The Court Case To Support Him
34	Letter To Trump Warning And Informing Him About The Destruction Of Our Nuclear Industry
35	Government Support To Islamic Terrorists
36	Massacre Of Parkland School Shooting
37	Rod Rosenstein Announced Indictments Of Russians In U.S. Election Meddling
38	Who Poisoned Sergei Skripal?
	Appendix
A	Exhibit 0: LIST OF EXHIBITS
B	The Internet Locations Of The Exhibits In List 0
C	Exhibit 10: SECOND LIST OF EXHIBITS
D	The Internet Locations Of The Exhibits In List 10

THE PURPOSE OF THIS BOOK

I want to make it clear to anyone that reads the book that I am biased to the truth and the wellbeing of America.

In this book, I am exposing the Political Prostitutes and the corrupt employees of the agencies of our government that their loyalty must had been to the People of this country, not to a certain political party, direction, or person. I demand the immediate firing of those employees and their supervisors up to the highest level that had the chance, position, or authority, to honestly serve the people, but failed, or refused pretending that there are regulations stopping them, or twisted our laws and Constitution to justify their carelessness. I demand the firing of all the lawyers that represented trump in this case (17cv2307) and all their supervisors including the Attorney General Jeff Sessions. I demand the immediate firing of all the FBI employees that were warned about the potential terrorists and failed to stop them including their supervisors up to the FBI directors.

INTRODUCTION TO THE THIRD EDITION

Originally, I published this book under the title "FARAG vs. TRUMP, TRIAL OF THE CENTURIES OF ISLAMIC SHARIA AND TERROR, THAT DISCLOSED THE NUCLEAR CRIME OF THE CENTURY", because I sued Trump and other officials in their official capacities, which should extend to reach Obama and his gang. However, I found out that this title is misrepresenting the nature of the book, which is to support Trump not to oppose him. Hence, I changed the title to reflect that my case was against Obama and the deep state, and kept almost everything in the book the same. Additionally, many people start realizing Obama's destruction to all our security agencies and infiltrating them with Islamic terrorists [https://www.youtube.com/watch?v=GqkZBWd6-nI].

It is very important to emphasize that my case against Islamic Sharia was never based on religious issues (according to the definition of a religion); it is based only on legal issues and facts.

The corruption, in almost every aspect of our system, had spread and increased dramatically, and even became legal in some cases, especially during Obama's presidency, in a way similar to the spread of prostitution. Abo-Elhak El-Hakani, in his book: "Can Trump Defeat Hillary, Obama, Islamic Terror, Prostituted Media, And Political Prostitution", said the following:

*"Prostitution is known as the engagement in sexual relations in exchange for money or some other benefit. People were engaged in prostitution to exchange benefits; the prostitute will gain financial benefits, and her customer will gain sexual pleasure. In some places, prostitution is legal. Similarly, in politics, we can see **politicians engaged in exchanges of benefits with their client**, whom I call "**Political Prostitutes**". In sexual prostitution, the prostitute is selling **only her own body**, but in Political Prostitution, the **politician is selling his country, his society, his position, the future of his people, and himself**. Also, the client is forced to **pay to get benefits and/or avoid harm**. Political prostitute is similar to a wife cheating on her husband and giving his property to her clients. Unfortunately, the USA is **saturated with political prostitutes** in every field. Some of them are **illegal prostitutes** and others are **amazingly legal***

*prostitutes, the most precarious of whom are the political representatives and the judges. The dangers of the political prostitutes increase in proportion to their ranks, and reach their climax when a **prostitute holds international position or deals with foreign rich countries**. Additionally, our political system is filled with **illegal** and **legal thieves**. A disaster will happen when a **political prostitute is also a thieve**.*"

I am going to expand the definition of that non-sexual prostitution to define the following words:

        Polistitute   : Prostituted Politician (Political Prostitute).
        Judgistitute : Prostituted Judge.
        Medistitute : Prostituted Media.

Every day passes and new facts appear, prove the allegations against the government, the Medistitute, and the Polistitutes. Trump recently made the remark that he looses in the lower courts but eventually wins in the Supreme Court, and then he asked a question if this **could tell something about our courts**?

After I published the first edition of this book, the USA's agencies continued and repeated their barrage of absurd actions and despicable failures. In the mean time, the Medistitute and the Polistitutes were rushing to justify and cover them. Two major things happened; the massacre of Parkland School Shooting on February 14, 2018, and the Rod Rosenstein Announcement of Indictments of Russians in U.S. Election Meddling, on February 16, 2018. I will comment on them on chapters 36 and 37. Then the British added their own unsupported accusations against the Russians that they tried to poison Sergei Skripal, and most the European countries and the U.S. followed them blindly, which I am going to analyze to show who did it.

INTRODUCTION

Notes:
- For the reader that wants to know the facts quickly, should focus on the chapter of the Second Amended Complaint, and the ones following it.

- This book is not written in the traditional way for literature, it follows the legal arguments in making concise and precise statements stating the facts, and avoiding conclusions of law.

After President Trump issued his executive order to ban the entrance of citizens of certain countries, although the order did not have any mention of Islam, voices were raised that his intentions were to ban Muslims from coming to the USA. As I am very fluent in Arabic language, and studied the real Islam and Sharia from their original Arabic sources, I realized that the executive order should have come with explicit banning of Sharia and violent Muslims, which would not violate the Muslims' freedom of religion, as explained in this book. At that time, I wanted to join the court cases against President Trump, to be on his side and explicitly ban Sharia and violent Muslims, but it was too late.

Under my misunderstanding that the courts have the power to explain the laws, I filed my case number 17cv02307, in the Federal Court in Chicago by myself (pro se), demanding a jury trial. To get the general criteria that would not qualify a religion to the freedom of religion according to our Constitution and laws, to apply to any religion without being accused of bias against any religion especially Islam, I asked the court to define these elements. This request was stated in paragraph 1 of the original complaint as:
1. Plaintiff seeks an Order declaring the elements that exclude a religion from the constitutional protection and ban its members from practicing it or entering the USA; compel the defendants to enforce our immigration laws; enjoin the Government Officials from admitting the president of Egypt or any other official from other countries that violates the freedom of religion; compensate Plaintiff for his damages; and for other relief.
However, I discovered that this is not the way our courts work; we have to have an ongoing issue that the court can examine. Accordingly, I asked the court to amend the complaint, the court granted my request, and I filed my first amended complaint.

In my first amended complaint, I stated explicitly the teachings of Sharia, the actions of Islamic terrorists, and the root causes of their terror. I asked the court to ban Sharia and violent Muslims, in addition to other relief. **It should be noted that the complaint is**

directed only to the incoming violent Muslims not the peaceful ones or the Muslims already inside the USA. The amended complaint stated the following:

a. Declare that Sharia is contrary to the Constitution and laws of the United States, and should be banned;
b. Issue an order enjoining the entrance of Muslims to the U.S. except those who denounce clearly and explicitly without deception, the teachings of Islam that do not comply with our Constitution or laws, and present their religious books clear from any incompliant, unlawful, or violent teachings;
c. Compel the Defendants to properly vet people entering the U.S.;
d. Enjoin Defendants from admitting Elsisi or any other foreign government official that committed violations of freedom of religion into the U.S.;
e. Compel Defendants to enforce our immigration laws;
f. Compensate the Plaintiff and his family for their damages.

During my legal research to support my case, I discovered that we have banning on uranium mining, and the companies working in this field are suffering, their stocks are deteriorating, and many of them are about to be bankrupt or already bankrupted. As a nuclear engineer, this was a surprising discovery that made me search our nuclear industry to discover more terrifying facts about how every element of our nuclear industry was destroyed by Hillary & Bill Clinton, Obama, and Obama's Administration.

Additionally, during the court proceedings, I discovered that the DOJ's lawyers that are representing President Trump and the government are trying to destroy Trump even if this will destroy the country. The names of the lawyers are:

1. CHAD A. READLER, Acting Assistant Attorney General, Civil Division
2. WILLIAM C. PEACHEY, Director, District Court Section, Office of Immigration Litigation.
3. JEFFREY S. ROBINS, Assistant Director, District Court Section, Office of Immigration Litigation.
4. AARON S. GOLDSMITH, Senior Litigation Counsel, District Court Section, U.S. Department of Justice.
5. JOEL R. LEVIN, Acting United States Attorney.
6. ALEX HARTZLER, Assistant United States Attorney.

7. HANS H. CHEN, Senior Litigation Counsel, U.S. Department of Justice, Civil Division, Office of Immigration Litigation.

I sent tens of complaints to President Trump, Secretary of State, Attorney General, and Chief of Staff, warning them, but I did not receive any response

After the discoveries of the nuclear crime and the targeting of President Trump, I asked the court to amend the complaint the second time, which the court agreed and I filed my second amended complaint.

Although my case is a civil one, my second amended complaint included many allegations of criminal activities that needed criminal prosecution. In the second amended complaint, I asked the court for the following:
I. Declare that Sharia is incompatible and contrary to the Constitution and laws of the United States, and should be banned;
II. Enjoin the application of Sharia in all the USA;
III. Enjoin the people that believe in Sharia from entering the USA;
IV. Issue an order enjoining the entrance of Muslims to the U.S. except those peaceful ones who denounce clearly and explicitly without deception, the teachings of Islam that do not comply with our Constitution or laws, and present their religious references clean from any incompliant, unlawful, or violent teachings;
V. Compel President Donald Trump to reissue his executive order to better protect the country;
VI. Compel the Defendants to enforce our immigration laws;
VII. Compel the Defendants to vet the people entering the USA to make sure that they do not endanger our wellbeing;
VIII. Enjoin Defendants from admitting Elsisi (President of Egypt) or any other foreign government official that committed violations of freedom of religion into the USA;
IX. Compensate Plaintiff at least $1,800,000,000.00 for destroying his business by the Russian-Uranium deal that destroyed our nuclear industry;
X. Compensate the Plaintiff and his family for their damages;
XI. Nullify all the actions of Obama and his administration that were biased to Islam.

I was shocked beyond any disbelief when the judge stopped the case from going to trial by dismissing it. **The unbelievable reason was that:**

I AM SEEKING RELIEF THAT WILL BENEFIT THE PUBLIC THE SAME WAY IT WILL BENEFIT ME.

The court ignored my allegations and dismissed my complaint for the strangest untrue reason that I do not have the right to sue (standing), because <u>my injuries are like the injuries of people at large</u>, which <u>violated the basic legal principles of the right to resolve ones grievance by court</u>. This dismissal will prevent the case from going to trial on the alleged facts, which will hide those facts from the public.

I filed a motion to reconsider, in which I explained the errors of the court, and asked it to reconsider its order dismissing the complaint, or in the alternative allow Counts I to IV and grant a writ of certiorari to the Supreme Court to resolve the issue of standing. However, the court quickly denied it.

One of my choices was to appeal the dismissal to the Appellate Court. Considering the political direction of the court in Chicago, there will be a very high probability to affirm the dismissal. After which I can appeal to the Supreme Court. I believe that I have a good chance of success in the Supreme Court, but my chance to let it examine the case is very slim. Therefore, I decided to let the people know the facts of the case and let them be the real judges.

This book will have all the relevant documents filed in the case in the same text including the spelling and grammatical errors.

I NAMED THIS BOOK "- - TRIAL OF THE CENTURIES OF ISLAMIC SHARIA - - ", BECAUSE I BELIEVE THAT THIS TRIAL **SHOULD HAVE HAPPENED CENTURIES** EARLIER

As for the exhibits that are part of the case, I will try to include the links for the references if they were available on the internet, and in case that any reference was removed from its link, the reader can refer to the one filed in court, which anyone can get as a public record.

I hope that this book will **help the victims of Islamic terror** understand some legal issues, <u>in case they wanted to pursue compensation for their damages</u>. However, this book is not a legal advice or to replace the help or the services of competent lawyers.

NOW WE COME TO THE FOLLOWING FACTS:

- WE THE CITIZENS, ESTABLISHED OUR GOVERNMENT AGENCIES AND ARE PAYING FOR THEIR SALARIES AND TOOLS, TO ENFORCE OUR LAWS AND PROTECT US.
- WE THE CITIZENS, ESTABLISHED A HUGE DEPARTMENT CALLED "DEPARTMENT OF JUSTICE", WITH TENS OF THOUSANDS OF LAWYERS TO DEFEND THE CITIZENS' RIGHTS AND DO WHAT ITS NAME IMPLIES.
- INSTEAD OF DOING THEIR JOBS, THEY KEEP ASKING FOR MORE MONEY AND RESOURCES.
- DUE TO THE GROSS NEGLIGENCE OF THOSE AGENCIES, MANY CITIZENS LOST THEIR LIVES, SUFFERED INJURIES INCLUDING SERIOUS PSYCHOLOGICAL DAMAGE, HUGE FINANCIAL LOSSES, DEPRIVATION OF THEIR HUMAN RIGHTS, AND OUR SOCIETY IS DEVASTATED.
- WHEN WE THE CITIZENS, INVOKE OUR SYSTEM TO REMEDY THE EFFECTS OF THE NEGLIGENCE OF OUR AGENCIES, WE DISCOVER THAT OUR DOJ IS QUICK TO BURST IN OUR FACES DECLARING THAT NO ONE HAS THE RIGHT FOR ANY COMPENSATION BECAUSE ALL OF US ARE SCREWED.
- WHAT KIND OF SOCIETY IS THIS? WHAT KIND OF SLAVES TO WHAT KIND OF MASTERS ARE WE?

1. THE ORIGINAL COMPLAINT

UNITED STATES DISTRICT COURT
NORTHERN DISTRICT OF ILLINOIS, EASTERN DIVISION

TAREK FARAG Plaintiff, v.	**Civil Action No**
DONALD J. TRUMP, in his official capacity as President of the United States; U.S. DEP. OF HOMELAND SECURITY; JOHN KELLY, in his official capacity as Secretary of Homeland Security; U.S. DEPARTMENT OF STATE; REX TILLERSON, in his official capacity as Secretary of State; the UNITED STATES OF AMERICA; and OTHER UNKNOWN DEFENDANTS. Defendants.	**17 CV 02307** Judge: **GARY FEINERMAN** Magistrate Judge: **SUSAN COX**

COMPLAINT FOR DECLARATORY, INJUNCTIVE, AND OTHER RELIEF

NATURE OF THE CASE

1. Plaintiff seeks an Order declaring the elements that exclude a religion from the constitutional protection and ban its members from practicing it or entering the USA; compel the defendants to enforce our immigration laws; enjoin the Government Officials from admitting the president of Egypt or any other official from other countries that violates the freedom of religion; compensate Plaintiff for his damages; and for other relief.

JURISDICTION AND VENUE

2. This Court has Federal Jurisdiction under 28 USC § 1331, the Administrative Procedure Act ("APA"), the Immigration and Nationality Act ("INA"), and other statutes.

3. The Court is authorized to award the requested declaratory, injunctive, and other relief under 28 USC §§ 2201-2202, and the APA, 5 USC § 706.

4. Venue is proper in this District pursuant to 28 USC § 1391.

INTRODUCTION

5. Tarek Farag, a US Citizen, brings this action to protect himself, family, and society; from the **intentional and unintentional negligence** of the defendants and other **unknown defendants** in **enforcing our laws, protecting our constitution, and protecting the wellbeing** of all citizens.

6. The miserable failures of the defendants to protect the country as demonstrated by the attacks of terrorists and losses of lives, made him feel **unsafe**, **terrified**, and **costing** him a lot of **time** and **money**. For example, when he flies he pays money to the government to torture him in long and time-consuming security lines, and allow strangers to humiliate him and invade his privacy.

7. People are confused about the **EXISTING limitations** and **EXCEPTIONS** of the Freedom of Religion under the Constitution, which does not give absolute protection to religions just because they call themselves religions, **they must comply with the Constitution and the Laws**.

8. Our Legislators enacted Immigration Laws that the President cannot override by executive orders, and <u>must enforce them</u> especially <u>against</u> the ones that **break them** (illegal immigrants).

9. There is news that Elsisi, the president of Egypt, is coming to the USA to discuss with the defendants ways to fight Terrorism, while he supports ISIS and **persecutes Christians** in Egypt.

CAUSES OF ACTION

COUNT I LIMITATIONS ON THE FREE EXERCISE OF RELIGION

10. 42 US Code § 2000bb–1 guarantee the free exercise of religion, with the exception only if the government demonstrates that application of the burden to the person (1) is in furtherance of a compelling governmental interest; and (2) is the least restrictive means - - - - - -.

11. Any <u>ideology or religion</u> (hereinafter <u>Belief</u>) that its teachings adopts, supports, or promotes <u>just one element</u> of the following, are against our Constitution and laws and should be banned:

    1) Forcing others (or its converts) to join their Belief by: murder, violence, expulsion, financial pressure, protection taxes, or deprivation of their human or constitutional rights.

    2) Depriving others from their religious freedom, which include but not limited to: harshly criticizing, analyzing, disputing, joining or leaving **any Belief**; worshiping, preaching, praying, practicing, possession and distribution of religious literature, or establishing places of assembly or prayer according to **their own Belief**.

    3) Any acts of: detention, interrogation, imposition of an onerous financial penalty, forced labor, forced mass resettlement, imprisonment, forced religious conversion, forcibly compelling non-believers or non-theists to recant their beliefs or to convert, beating, torture, mutilation, rape, enslavement, murder, and execution.

    4) **<u>Discriminating against others</u>** based on religion, origin, gender, etc.

    5) Having **<u>contradicting teachings</u>** (e.g. teaches in one part to kill the disbelievers and in other part teaches to love and make peace with the disbelievers).

    6) **<u>Using deception</u>** and misrepresentation of its teachings to spread its Belief.

12. A person declaring that he/she **will not practice**, the teachings of **his BELIEF** that are **INCOMPLIANT** with our Constitution and laws, should be banned, because this will make him/her a potential hidden member of that Belief. E.g., we cannot allow a person saying that he is a Nazi to practice Nazism by accepting his swearing that he is not a racist or anti-Semitic. A Nazi is a Nazi, <u>no such thing as moderate Nazi, extreme Nazi, or partially Nazi</u>.

13. Not clarifying the above limitations clearly, allowed people that should have been banned from practicing their Belief and from entering the US caused serious harm to the citizens, which caused

Farag loss of money and continuous fear for his life, family, property, and community.

COUNT II TRUMP IS PLANNING TO ADMIT ELSISI VIOLATING THE LAW

14. 8 US Code § 1182(G) prevent the admission of foreign government officials who have committed particularly severe **violations of religious freedom**.

15. The defendants are inviting Elsisi, the president of Egypt, to a meeting in the USA.

16. Elsisi came to power after his military coupe in Egypt. He formed a team, mostly of extreme Islamists, to enact an Islamic Constitution that discriminates against non-Muslims and declares Egypt an Islamic country, and Islamic Sharia law is the superior law above the Constitution.

17. Lately, Elsisi enacted Sharia Law rules that restrict the repairs of Churches or building of new ones, while pretending to give Christians more freedom to do so.

18. Following are some of the sufferings of Christians that Elsisi ignored or encouraged:

    a) A group of lawyers presented to Elsisi a file containing more than 500 cases of criminal kidnappings (under the Egyptian code) of Christian **UNDERAGE** girls that were forced to Islam and to **MARRY** Moslems. Elsisi refused to take any action because Sharia Law prohibits these girls from converting from Islam, they now joined the best religion (Islam) and it is in their best interest not to become Infidels. They must stay away from their families **forever** to avoid their pressure, irrespective of **being underage**.

    b) In one day, about 80 Churches were looted and burned, along with tens of Christian homes and businesses. Up until now, no victim was compensated, and no perpetrator was questioned or arrested in spite of the overwhelming evidence against them.

    c) Three children (ages under 14) were sentenced to 3 years in prison plus huge financial penalty for producing a short video clip mocking ISIS. An Islamic judge considered the video **insulting to Islam because it showed some of its facts**. After few seconds from calling the case, and without trial, the Judge ordered their immediate imprisonment without posting bonds (against the rules) and without waiting for the order to be final.

d) On May 20, 2016, in the village of AlKarm (Minya-Egypt), a mob of more than 300 armed Moslems attacked, looted, burned the homes of Christian families, and stripped naked an old woman and paraded her in the street,. The police arrested the five Christian victims and 1 Moslem man, and the victimized families were expelled from the village.

e) In December 2016, an explosion in Cairo Cathedral killed and injured more than 100. Many believe that the security forces orchestrated it to blame Islamic terrorists to show that Elsisi is fighting terror. Elsisi ordered the authorities to close the investigations and the army to repair the Cathedral quickly to **destroy the evidence**.

f) Elsisi pardoned 200 imprisoned terrorists ignoring tens of unjustly jailed Christians.

g) In February 2017, many Christians were brutally killed (burned alive in front of their families) in the city of El Arish (Sinai-Egypt). Both the police and the army **refused to protect Christians**, forcing the expulsion of more than 100 families from the city.

19. Elsisi as a military man and a leader of the intelligence apparatus supports the Islamic terror, while **playing its card** by pretending to fight it. It is impossible for Trump to rely on Elsisi to fight terrorism, knowing that the Egyptian military is devoting most of its resources to invest in the civilian sector hoping to increase its share in **Egypt's GDP to more than 55%**.

20. From the above, it is immoral, useless, and in violation of the law to admit Elsisi to the USA. The Court should enjoin Defendants from inviting Elsisi or admitting him to the USA.

COUNT III   COMPEL THE DEFENDANTS TO ENFORCE OUR LAWS

21. Plaintiff migrated to the USA about 30 years ago. He waited 10 years to get his turn plus 5 years to become a citizen, to be able to file applications for the immigration of his family members, which allowed these families to migrate after about 15 years from applying.

22. These families' turn to migrate came after about 20 years from the immigration of Plaintiff. The parents of these families were close to the retirement age, most of their children passed the age of 21, and could not migrate with their parents. As a result, one family abandoned the migration. The parents only of the second family migrated, but were divided between staying in the USA and visiting their children that most of them had children. The parents of the third family came to the USA with two of their children leaving one, but could not stay as one family and the parents returned with one child leaving one child to study and work to support himself.

23. Plaintiff believe that a reason for <u>depriving these families from their legal rights to migrate according to the law</u>, is that the USA is saturated with illegal immigrants that **<u>ILLEGALLY took their turns, caused the separation of these families, and loss of time and money</u>**.

24. DHS estimates the number of **illegal** immigrants in the USA to be close to **11 million**.

25. A respected country <u>would not knowingly allow one citizen to break any law for 1 minute</u>. **<u>Now we have a disaster of 11 million non-citizens, breaking the law</u>**, for **many years**, **stealing** the **rights** of legal immigrants, and **demanding** us to **change our laws to make them legal**.

26. Under Article II of the Constitution, the **President is responsible for the <u>execution and enforcement of the laws</u>** created by Congress, not to make executive orders to suspend the law.

27. The carelessness of the president in enforcing our laws inflicts ongoing harm upon Plaintiff, his family, legal immigrants, many families of legal immigrants, and the society.

28. The court should penalize the President and compel him to execute the law.

PRAYER FOR RELIEF

29. WHEREFORE, Plaintiff Tarek Farag prays that the Court:
    a. Declare that any ideology or religion that its teachings adopts, supports, or promotes just one element of any of the elements stated above in paragraphs 11 and 12, are contrary to the Constitution and laws of the United States, and its practice, and the admittance of its followers to the USA,

should be banned;

b. Grant Plaintiff a leave to amend his complaint;

c. Enjoin Defendants from admitting Elsisi in the USA, and cancel his visit;

d. Compel the President and the Defendants to execute our laws;

e. Compensate the Plaintiff and his family for their damages; and

f. Award such additional and other relief as this Court deems just.

Respectfully submitted,

Plaintiff: TAREK FARAG, pro se

Plaintiff: Tarek Farag
Date: March 27, 2017

2. NOTICE TO FILE INITIAL STATUS REPORT

Case: 1:17-cv-02307 Document #: 6 Filed: 03/30/17 Page 1 of 1 Page ID #:11

NOTIFICATION OF DOCKET ENTRY

This docket entry was made by the Clerk on Thursday, March 30, 2017:

MINUTE entry before the Honorable Gary Feinerman:Initial status hearing set for 5/25/2017 at 9:00 a.m. Initial Status Report shall be filed by 5/18/2017. Please see Judge Feinerman's web page (http://www.ilnd.uscourts.gov, to "District Judges," to "Judge Gary Feinerman," to "Initial Status Hearings" under Case Management Procedures) for details on the Initial Status Hearing and Initial Status Report. Mailed notice.(jlj,)

3. MOTION TO ENTER AN ORDER

MOTION FOR DECLARATORY ORDER SPECIFYING THE ELEMENTS OF AN IDEOLOGY OR A RELIGION THAT SHOULD RESULT IN BANNING IT

1. Plaintiff's complaint in Count I, seeks an Order declaring the elements that exclude a religion from the constitutional protection and bans its members from practicing it or entering the USA.

2. Venue is proper under 28 USC § 1391, and this Court has Jurisdiction under 28 USC § 1331, because this action is arising under the Constitution and Laws of the USA to declare the legal relations of the banning to them pursuant to 28 USC §§ 2201. Since the required declaration is not against any party, this Court can issue the decree on the pleading (28 USC §§ 2202).

3. The First Amendment protects the freedom of religions, while 42 USC § 2000bb–1 (b)(1) defines the limitations and exceptions on them in cases of conflict with governmental interests.

4. 8 USC § 1182 banns from entering the USA the persons who are: Opposed to, or to control or overthrow of, the Government of the US by **force, violence, or other unlawful means** (3)(A)(iii); or a **member of or affiliated with a totalitarian party** (3)(D)(i).

5. It is in the interest of the US Government to avoid any potential harm to it and its citizens by banning any ideology or religion (hereinafter Belief) that **its teachings adopts, supports, or promotes** any element that conflicts with our Constitution and laws, which includes but not limited to the following:

    1) **Forcing** people of other Belief or its converts to join their Belief by **murder, violence, expulsion, financial pressure, protection taxes, or deprivation of their liberty or security**.

    2) Depriving others from their religious freedom, which includes but not limited to: **harshly criticizing, analyzing,**

23

disputing, joining or leaving **any Belief**; worshiping, preaching, praying, practicing, possession and distribution of religious literature, or establishing places of assembly or prayer according to **their own Belief**.

3) Any acts of: detention, interrogation, imposition of an onerous financial penalty, forced labor, forced mass resettlement, imprisonment, forced religious conversion, forcibly compelling non-believers or non-theists to recant their beliefs or to convert, beating, torture, mutilation, rape, enslavement, murder, and execution.

4) **Discriminating against others** based on religion, origin, gender, etc.

5) Having violent **contradicting teachings** (e.g. teaches in one part to be violent against certain people and in other parts teaches to love and make peace with the same people).

6) **Using deception, subterfuge, and misrepresentation** of its teachings to spread its Belief.

7) Having **totalitarian** teachings.

8) Using **force, violence, or other unlawful means to achieve their goals.**

9) Not giving men and women of full age, equal rights to marry with their free and full consent without any limitation due to religion, race, gender, or nationality.

6. A person who has a certain Belief of which some of its teachings incite violence must be banned. However, he/she is free to make up his/her own Belief, or adopt others Belief, with the conditions that its teachings are published, and has no secretive violent teachings. For example, if we are banning the practice of Nazism, we cannot allow a person saying that he is a Nazi to practice Nazism by accepting his swearing that he is not a racist. A Nazi is a Nazi, no such thing as moderate Nazi, extreme Nazi, or partially Nazi.

7. Failure to clarify the above limitations to the freedom of Belief, allowed people that should have been banned from practicing their Belief to enter the US, and caused serious harm to its citizens, which caused plaintiff Farag loss of money and continuous fear for his life, family, property, and community.

8. WHEREFORE, Plaintiff Tarek Farag prays that this Court:
   a. Declare that any ideology or religion that its teachings adopts, supports, or promotes any of the elements stated

above in paragraphs 4, 5, or 6, are contrary to the laws and Constitution of the United States, its practice is banned, and its followers are banned from entering the USA;
b. Grant Plaintiff a leave to amend his complaint; and
c. Award such additional and other relief as this Court deems just.

        Respectfully submitted,

                              /S/ TAREK FARAG

Date: April 21, 2017

4- ORDER DENYING THE MOTION TO ENTER AN ORDER

Case: 1:17-cv-02307 Document #: 16 Filed: 04/24/17 Page 1 of 1 Page ID #:29

NOTIFICATION OF DOCKET ENTRY

This docket entry was made by the Clerk on Monday, April 24, 2017:

MINUTE entry before the Honorable Gary Feinerman: Plaintiff's motion for declaratory order specifying the elements of an ideology or a religion that should result in banning it [14] is denied without prejudice. Putting aside other possible obstacles to the relief he seeks, Plaintiff's motion does not establish that Defendants have admitted into the United States any person barred by 8 U.S.C. 1182(a)(3)(A)(iii) or 1182(a)(3)(D)(i). Motion hearing set for 4/26/2017 [15] is stricken. Mailed notice.(jlj,)

ATTENTION: This notice is being sent pursuant to Rule 77(d) of the Federal Rules of Civil Procedure or Rule 49(c) of the Federal Rules of Criminal Procedure. It was generated by CM/ECF, the automated docketing system used to maintain the civil and criminal dockets of this District. If a minute order or other document is enclosed, please refer to it for additional information.

For scheduled events, motion practices, recent opinions and other information, visit our web site at *www.ilnd.uscourts.gov*.

5. MOTION TO RECONSIDER AND AMEND

MOTION TO AMEND THE COMPLAINT

1. Plaintiff's original complaint asked the Court to declare the elements that exclude a religion or ideology from the constitutional protection, and bans its members from practicing it or entering the USA, from a **neutral standpoint without directing it to a specific religion or ideology** (the **Court** will **say what the law** is). Plaintiff asked for leave to amend the complaint, so that he can **seek specific relieves against proper parties WITHIN this declaratory order, AFTER it is issued to save time and resources**.

2. Around 4/21/17, Plaintiff filed a motion for that declaratory order (as in ¶1), stating 8 USC 1182 as one **example of an already existing ban**, not to establish claim against anyone, or seek relief against any party. Plaintiff's motion intended to have the Court **define** the existing **Constitution and laws as to the banning**. The Court denied it without prejudice on 4/24/17, because Plaintiff's motion did not establish that Defendants have admitted into the US any person barred by 8 USC 1182.

3. Plaintiff believes that declaring and defining the elements as to banning, which he requested in his motion of 4/21/17, will help reduce the litigation. Because once the rules are clear ahead of pursuing any relief against any party, the validity of a claim will be easy to determine, which will help avoid filing and arguing bad pleadings.

4. Amending the complaint early before the defendants file their response, will help reduce the burden on them.

5. WHEREFORE, Plaintiff Tarek Farag prays that this Court:
a. Reconsider its denial of his motion of 4/21/17, and define the existing Constitution and laws as to the banning;

b. Grant Plaintiff a leave to amend his complaint; and
c. Award such additional and other relief as this Court deems just.
    Respectfully submitted,
          /S/ TAREK FARAG

6. COURT ORDER DENYING THE MOTION TO RECONSIDER AND GRANTING LEAVE TO AMEND

Case: 1:17-cv-02307 Document #: 20 Filed: 05/01/17 Page 1 of 1 Page ID # 35

NOTIFICATION OF DOCKET ENTRY

This docket entry was made by the Clerk on Monday, May 1, 2017:

MINUTE entry before the Honorable Gary Feinerman: Motion to amend and reconsider [18] is granted in part and denied in part. Plaintiff may file an amended complaint by 5/15/2017. The court will not reconsider the denial [16] of of Plaintiff's prior motion [14]. Motion hearing set for 5/3/2017 [19] is stricken. Mailed notice. (jlj,)

7. AMENDED COMPLAINT

AMENDED COMPLAINT

Note: Attached are 9 exhibits, listed in Exhibit 0.
To refer to exhibits, the expression "Please refer to Exhibit 3c page 23" is stated as [E3cp23], and "see Exhibit 2" as [E2].

INTRODUCTION

1. Plaintiff brings this action to protect his life, family, property, and community against the Islamic terrorists that should have been banned from entering or promoting their ideologies in the U.S.
2. Defendants have a duty to protect the citizens of the USA from dangerous individuals entering the U.S. with a belief system that gives them the right to kill or terrorize its citizens.
3. Defendants were negligent in their duties, they knew and/or should have known, that Sharia (Islamic Sharia Law) is incompatible with our Constitution and laws, and must be banned.
4. Plaintiff seeks an order declaring that **Sharia is incompatible** with our laws and constitution, and must be banned.
5. Plaintiff seeks an order **enjoining Muslims from entering the US**, except those who **denounce clearly, explicitly, and without deception, the teachings of Islam that do not comply with our Constitution or laws, and PRESENT THEIR RELIGIOUS BOOKS clear from any incompliant, unlawful, or violent teachings**.
6. Plaintiff seeks an order to compel the defendants to vet people entering the US to make sure that they do not adopt, practice, or promote a violent ideology or religion.
7. Plaintiff seeks an order to compel the defendants to **enforce our immigration laws**.
8. Plaintiff seeks an order to enjoin the government officials from **admitting** the president of Egypt or any other official from other countries that **violates the freedom of religion**.

JURISDICTION AND VENUE

9. This Court has Federal Jurisdiction under 28 USC § 1331, the Administrative Procedure Act ("APA"), the Immigration and Nationality Act ("INA"), and other statutes.
10. The Court is authorized to award the requested declaratory, injunctive, and other relief under 28 USC §§ 2201-2202, and the APA, 5 USC § 706.
11. Venue is proper in this District pursuant to 28 USC § 1391.

ARGUMENT

12. Plaintiff Tarek Farag is a US Citizen of Egyptian descent lived in the US for three decades.
13. Farag finished his PhD work in Nuclear Engineering in 1988, while he was in Egypt, and migrated with his family since then to the US.
14. Farag and his wife have four children. They are U.S. citizens and live in different states.
15. Sharia law is Islam's legal system. It is derived from the Quran, Hadith (statements of the prophet Mohammad), and Sera (biography of Mohammad). It is a collection of Islam's teachings and is **mandated** on **every Muslim to follow and apply it everywhere and all the times**. We need to **notice the difference between Islam** as an ideology, and **Muslims as humans** that are **no different** from any other humans, but **their behavior can change according to Islam's teachings**. In other words, **we should not have problems with Muslims as humans**, but we **could have problems with the teachings of Islam**.
16. Sharia teaches the beheading of the non-Muslims, expelling them, seizing their property, and taking their women and children as slaves [E1p72].
17. Sharia orders its followers to hate the non-Muslims and to be brutally violent against them [E1p65], [E3cp118].
18. Islam's ultimate goal is to wage Jihad war against all non-Muslims to eliminate them until the entire world becomes Islamic [E1p78].
19. Islam practices human sacrifice to please God by killing (beheading) non-Muslims, which is rewarded in life by looting their properties and enslaving their women and children, and after

death by going to heaven [E1p80].

20. **No freedom of religion in Islam for anyone**, Muslims or non-Muslims, and Islam insults all other religions and criminalizes them [E1p65]. The **death penalty** is enacted for: Muslim men not praying regularly [E3bcp35,82,93,130,132]; converts from Islam [E3cp27], [E1p76]; anyone insulting or criticizing Islam or preaching for any religion other than Islam [E1p74], [E3cp27]; **Muslim men capable of jihad and not joining it** [E1p97]; and non-Muslims not paying gizia ("protection tax" to protect non-Muslims from Muslims) [E3cp27].

21. Christians and Jews are allowed to exist in Islamic societies under very harsh and humiliating conditions to force them to convert to Islam or leave the country. They may not build or repair their places of worship even if the Khalifa permitted them, and Christians should not install bells, towers for bells, outside visible Crosses or Churches, or have a Church higher than a mosque [E3cp116]. All other non-Muslims are considered Koffar (infidels) and must be killed.

22. Islam had peaceful teachings at its start when it had few followers, not enough to use violence to force people to join it. The prophet Mohammad decided to build an army from professional fighters that their only job was to fight to force people to join Islam and increase the wealth of Muslims under the name of Jihad [E1p86]. To justify the looting of the wealth of the non-Muslims, Islam reversed all its peaceful teachings to become very violent against non-Muslims, which Islam considers them improvements and abrogation [E1p65]. Muslims use these conflicting teachings in deceiving their enemies by presenting the peaceful teachings until they feel safe, and then Muslims surprise them with the opposite violent teachings that call for their elimination [E1p88]. At the very least, people will live and deal with Muslims, under the mercy of their whims not knowing which teachings they will apply.

23. Islam prohibits non-Muslims from imitating Moslems in their dress, appearance, carrying weapons, riding horses, growing their hair or beard, etc. and must mark themselves in a way to know easily that they are not Muslims [E3cp117]. This is why Muslims insist on Islamic dresses and fight to impose their dress code (like the Burkini war), especially in foreign countries, to distinguish themselves from non-Muslims [E1p42].

24. Islam applies different rules for non-Muslims to prefer Muslims. For example, the financial compensation for the wrongful death (Deya) of a free Christian woman is about 16.7% of that for a free Muslim man, and 0% for an atheist man (he should be killed anyway) [E1p61].

25. Islam mandates its followers to show their superiority and humiliate others [E3cp118].

26. Islam allows its followers to kill other humans and eat them when they can not find food, which is ISIS is doing in besieged places (they even save them until they need to eat) [E3cp131].

27. Islam interferes with the enforcement of the law and disregards it, and mandates Muslims to act by themselves whenever they feel Sharia rules were violated [E1p65].

28. Islam allows Muslims to use deception to hide their identity and intentions to enforce, spread, and favor Islam, and eliminate other religions (Taqyiah principle) [E1p68]. One example is the **deception of the Grand Imam of Al-Azhar** (Alazhar is the oldest authority in Islamic teachings in the world) when he addressed the German Parliament on March 16, 2016, in an attempt to draw a good picture of Islam in the western countries [E1p118].

29. Islam requires Muslims to follow the prophet Mohammad as the best model [E1p71].

30. Islam does not equate women with men: a) all women are deficient in their brain and religion, and their guile is very great; b) a woman's compensation for wrongful death is half of a man; c) a woman's testimony is half of a man; d) a woman may not be a judge or hold a leading position; e) men are in charge of women and should beat them if they disobeyed them; and f) a man can marry up to 4 women in addition to unlimited enslaved women from jihad, while women cannot have more than one husband or she must be killed [E1p92].

31. Islam has death punishment for homosexuality [E1p94].

32. Muslims are **using the tolerance of non-Islamic countries to invade** them by immigrants to spread the intolerance of Islam [E1p98]. After the massacre of Charlie Hebdo attack, a huge demonstration of British Muslims gathered in London to protest, **not to condemn the Islamic terror and the perpetrators of the massacre**, but **to condemn the victims**, and provided a petition signed by more than 100,000 British Muslims calling for the exceptional respect for Islam [E1p135].

33. ISIL, ISIS, Boko Haram, Elshabab, DAESH, Moslem Brotherhood, Al Qaeda, etc. represent the true teachings of Islam; they are not radicals or extremists [E1p99].
34. Islam is Islam, there is no such thing as moderate Islam, radical Islam, or cute Islam [E1p100].
35. Former president Obama, violated the First Amendment to the United Sstates Constitution by promoting Islam as the Religion of Peace and supported the Islamic terror in Syria and the Middle East with weapons, finances, military training, and political support via our tax dollars.
36. The US Government and its Agencies **IGNORED the warnings about the Muslim terrorists of the "Boston Marathon"**, and failed miserably to protect the citizens. **In defending Islam, DOJ** (Department of Justice) **insisted that this terror is politically motivated and not an Islamic terror, which is not true**.
37. As if the massacre of the "Boston Marathon" by **Muslims**, was not enough to wake up our government, it **ignored another warning about "San Bernardino" massacre** by **Muslims**, which again was not enough and **ignored another warning about "Orlando Florida" massacre by Muslim**. I believe that any person can conclude that **these failures are intentional**; considering the billions of dollars spent on all those security agencies, the unlimited resources they have, and their spying power on the US citizens.
38. Upon information from JW (Judicial Watch), the Obama administration was the first in history to dispatch a US Attorney General to personally reassure Muslims that the DOJ is dedicated to protecting them [E7].
39. In an unprecedented event, Attorney General Eric Holder assured a San Francisco-based organization (Muslim Advocates) that urges members not to cooperate in federal terrorism investigations that the "us versus them" environment created by the U.S. government, law enforcement agents, and fellow citizens is "**unacceptable and inconsistent with what America is all about**" [E7].
40. JW found that the Obama administration had embarked on a fervent crusade to befriend Muslims by creating a variety of outreach programs at a number of key federal agencies. For instance, Homeland Security covertly met with a group of extremist Arab, Muslim and Sheikh organizations to discuss national security matters and the State Department sent a controversial, anti-America

Imam (Feisal Abdul Rauf) to the Middle East to foster greater understanding and outreach among Muslim majority communities. The Obama Administration has also hired a special Homeland Security adviser (Mohamed Elibiary) who openly supports a radical Islamist theologian, renowned jihadist ideologue, and a special Islam envoy that condemns U.S. prosecutions of terrorists as "politically motivated persecutions" and has close ties to radical extremist groups. Obama even ordered the National Aeronautics and Space Administration (NASA) to shift its mission from space exploration to Muslim diplomacy [E7].

41. Former Secretary of State Hillary Clinton allowed the reentry of two radical Islamic academics whose terrorist ties have long banned them from the U.S [E8].

42. The Obama DOJ threatened that spreading information considered inflammatory against Muslims could constitute a violation of civil rights, which is a violation of First Amendment [E7].

43. The Obama Administration adopted UN resolution 16/18 (an initiative of the Organization of Islamic Cooperation), which limit speech that is viewed as "discriminatory" or which involves the "defamation of religion" specifically that which can be viewed as "incitement to imminent violence". This is a violation of the First Amendment intended to promote Islam [E9].

44. The Federal government is prohibited from involving itself in religion, but the DOJ acted on behalf of Islam in many court cases wasting our resources (e.g. case number 15 C 8628).

45. The Obama administration ignored the **massacres against Christians** and non-Muslims in Iraq and Syria, and **waited until they were decimated**, and then rushed in **pretending** to take action and offered ten thousand Syrians (some claims that they are 200,000) asylums to enter the US. It proved to be an obvious **biased move favoring Muslims**, because the percentage of Christians refugees was less than 1% while their ratio in Syria was about 10% (**1,000% bias** ratio, which indicates a **blockade on Christians**).

46. Obama misrepresented the number of victims of Islamic terrorists stating that the majority are Muslims, which proves again that the source of this terror is Islam itself. This fact was obvious from the brutalities and terror between both Shia and Sunni Muslims that share the same ideology. While the Christian victims were

35

targeted because they were Christians, and they have nowhere to escape.

47. Judicial Watch announced that it obtained 183 pages of documents from the Department of Homeland Security revealing that the Obama administration scrubbed the law enforcement agency's "Terrorist Screening Database" in order to protect what it considered the civil rights of suspected Islamic terrorist groups. The documents **appear to confirm charges that Obama** administration changes created a massive "hands off" list. Removed data from the terrorist watch list **could have helped prevent the San Bernardino terrorist attack** [E4], [E6].

48. Obama administration officials refused to appear before Congress to explain the decision to purge all references to "Islamic terrorism" and radicalism from public documents [E5].

CAUSES OF ACTION

COUNT I DECLARATORY RELIEF THAT SHARIA IS INCOMPATIBLE WITH OUR LAWS AND CONSTITUTION, AND SHOULD BE BANNED

49. The foregoing ¶1 to ¶48 are realleged and incorporated by reference herein as ¶49.

50. 42 US Code § 2000bb–1 guarantee the free exercise of religion, **with the exception** only if the government demonstrates that application of the burden to the person (1) is in furtherance of a compelling governmental interest; and (2) is the least restrictive means - - - - - -.

51. The Declaratory Judgment Act, in relevant part, provides: "In a case of actual controversy within its jurisdiction ... any court of the United States, upon the filing of an appropriate pleading, may declare the rights and other legal relations of any interested party seeking such declaration, whether or not further relief is or could be sought". Passage of the Act was intended "to prevent avoidable damages from being incurred by a person uncertain of his rights and threatened with damage by delayed adjudication". The availability of declaratory relief is limited, moreover, by Article III of the Constitution, which restricts judicial power to the adjudication of "Cases" or "Controversies". To obtain a declaratory judgment relief the dispute has to be "immediate" and "real".

52. Defendants have a duty to protect the citizens of the USA from dangerous individuals entering the US with a believe system that they have the right to kill or terrorize its citizens that do not adhere to Islamic principles.

53. Defendants were negligent in their duties, they knew and/or should have known the dangers of allowing those dangerous individuals to enter the US and terrorize the country.

54. From the above allegations, there are real great dangers from allowing people that believe in **Sharia** to enter the U.S. and commit terrorists' **acts that are impossible to completely stop** or **reverse**. Currently, we have fights over Trump's Executive Orders to ban Muslims from entering the U.S. without proper vetting, and his predecessor's unconstitutional acts to allow potential Muslim terrorists to enter as refugees. Additionally, we have areas in the U.S. where Muslims are imposing or try to impose Sharia, while others are banning it or trying to ban it. Hence, the Court should **issue immediately an Order Declaring That Sharia Is Incompatible with Our Laws and Constitution and Should Be Banned**.

COUNT II INJUNCTIVE RELIEF BANNING THE ENTRANCE OF MUSLIMS IN THE U.S. EXCEPT UNDER CERTAIN CONDITIONS

55. The foregoing ¶1 to ¶54 are realleged and incorporated by reference herein as ¶55.

56. From the above allegations we can see that Muslims must follow Sharia or get killed, they have no choice not to participate in jihad, they can use deception to hide their intentions, they must discriminate and be violent against non-Muslims, they must commit terrorists' acts, etc., which are all against our laws and Constitution.

57. **8 U.S. Code § 1182 (3) already does not allow the admission of the people that adopt or promote Sharia's principles**.

58. We are a country of immigrants. We welcome and select good people that want to enjoy our values and enrich our society. We are not a sanctuary for criminals and ideologies that want to destroy us. No one has a right to come to the U.S. (except our citizens or to become citizens according to our laws); we give this privilege to others that deserve it according to our laws. Hence, no one, including Muslims, **can claim** that he/she was deprived from a right

to enter the U.S. when we <u>practice our rights and duties to protect our citizens</u> from any potential harm **however minute**.

59. From the above argument, and watching the real events around the entire world; we should put the safety and the well-being of our citizens first and ban Muslims from entering the U.S., without owing any apology to anyone.

60. We can consider special cases for **Muslims that would respect our values, laws, and Constitution**, and want to enter the U.S., but they must be sincere in their intentions and <u>**denounce clearly and explicitly without deception, the teachings of Islam that do not comply with our Constitution or laws**</u>, and <u>**present their religious books clear from any incompliant, unlawful, or violent teachings**</u>.

COUNT III COMPEL THE DEFENDANTS TO VET THE PEOPLE ENTERING THE U.S. TO MAKE SURE THAT THEY DO NOT ENDANGER OUR WELLBEING

61. The foregoing ¶1 to ¶60 are realleged and incorporated by reference herein as ¶61.

62. The Obama administration was grossly negligent in admitting people from countries like Haiti without proper vetting, instead of helping them develop their countries.

63. The Obama administration aided the Islamic terrorists in destroying Syria and killing hundreds of thousands of innocent people. When the legitimate Syrian government started defeating them, the Obama administration rushed to bring to the U.S. Muslims only, with very few non-Muslims as a cover-up, without any vetting; endangering our country and in violation of our laws.

64. The Court should stop Defendants from endangering our country, and issue an Order to compel Defendants to properly vet people coming to the U.S.

COUNT IV IT IS A VIOLATION OF OUR LAWS TO ADMIT THE PRESIDENT OF EGYPT OR OTHER FOREIGN GOVERNMENT OFFICIALS WHO HAVE VIOLATED RELIGIOUS FREEDOM

65. The foregoing ¶1 to ¶64 are realleged and incorporated by reference herein as ¶65.

66. 8 US Code § 1182(G) prevents the admission of foreign government officials who have "committed particularly severe **violations of religious freedom**" into the U.S.

67. Defendants admitted Elsisi (President of Egypt) around the beginning of April 2017, into the U.S. knowing that he committed grave violations of religious freedom and human rights.

68. Elsisi came to power after his military coupe in Egypt. He formed a team, mostly of extreme Islamists, to enact an Islamic Constitution that discriminates against non-Muslims and declares Egypt an Islamic country, and Islamic Sharia law is the superior law above the Constitution.

69. Elsisi enacted Sharia Law rules that restrict the repairs of Churches or building of new ones, while claiming to give Christians more freedom to do so.

70. Following are some of the sufferings of Christians that Elsisi ignored and/or encouraged:

a) A group of lawyers presented to Elsisi a file containing more than **500 cases of criminal kidnappings** (under the Egyptian code) of Christian **UNDERAGE girls** that were forced to Islam and to **MARRY Moslems**. Elsisi refused to take any action because Sharia Law prohibits these girls from converting from Islam, they now joined the best religion (Islam) and it is in their best interest not to become Infidels. They must stay away from their families **forever** to avoid their pressure, irrespective of **being underage**.

b) In one day, approximately 80 Churches were looted and burned, along with tens of Christian homes and businesses. Up until now, no victim was compensated, and no perpetrator was questioned or arrested in spite of the overwhelming evidence.

c) Three children (ages under 14) were sentenced to 3 years in prison plus huge financial penalty for producing a short video clip mocking ISIS. An Islamic judge considered the video **insulting to Islam because it showed some of its facts**. Moments after calling the case, and without trial, the Judge ordered their immediate imprisonment without posting bonds (against the rules) and without waiting for the order to be final.

d) On May 20, 2016, in the village of AlKarm (Minya-Egypt), a mob of more than 300 armed Moslems attacked, looted, burned the homes of Christian families, and stripped naked an old woman and paraded her in the street,. The police arrested the five Christian victims and 1 Moslem man, and the victimized families were expelled from the village.

e) In December 2016, an explosion in Cairo Cathedral killed and injured more than 100. Many believe that the security forces orchestrated it to blame Islamic terrorists to show that Elsisi is fighting terror. Elsisi ordered the authorities to close the investigations and the army to repair the Cathedral quickly to **destroy the evidence**.

f) Elsisi pardoned 200 imprisoned terrorists ignoring tens of unjustly jailed Christians.

g) In February 2017, many Christians were brutally killed (burned alive in front of their families) in the city of El Arish (Sinai-Egypt). Both the police and the army **refused to protect Christians**, forcing the expulsion of more than 100 families from the city.

h) On April 9, 2017, Islamic terrorists that were known to the security agencies in Egypt bombed three Churches in the cities of Tanta and Alexandria killing and injuring hundreds of innocent Christians. However, Elsisi (he directs and controls everything including judges, media, elected officials, etc.) never prosecuted the people that organized these massacres or the ones that incited them, and never compensated the victims properly.

71. <u>Elsisi</u> as a military man and a leader of the intelligence apparatus <u>supports Islamic terror</u>, while **playing its card** by pretending to fight it. It is impossible for Trump to rely on Elsisi to fight terrorism, knowing that the <u>Egyptian military is devoting most of its resources to invest in the civilian sector hoping to increase its share in</u> **Egypt's GDP to more than 55%**.

72. From the above, it is immoral, useless, and in violation of the law to admit Elsisi to the U.S. The Court should **enjoin Defendants from admitting into the U.S., Elsisi or any foreign government official that violated the freedom of religion**.

COUNT V COMPEL THE DEFENDANTS TO ENFORCE OUR IMMIGRATION LAWS

73. The foregoing ¶1 to ¶72 are realleged and incorporated by reference herein as ¶73.

74. Plaintiff migrated to the USA about 30 years ago. He <u>waited 10 years to get his turn plus 5 years to become a citizen</u>, to be able to file applications for the immigration of his family members, which

allowed these families to migrate after about 15 years from applying.

75. These families' opportunity to migrate came after about 20 years from the immigration of Plaintiff. The parents of these families were nearing retirement age; most of their children passed the age of 21, and could not migrate with their parents. As a result, one family abandoned the migration. The parents only of the second family migrated, but were divided between staying in the USA and visiting their children that most of them had children. The parents of the third family came to the USA with two of their children leaving one, but could not stay as one family and the parents returned with one child leaving one child alone to study and work to support himself.

76. Plaintiff believes that a reason for **depriving these families from their legal rights to migrate according to the law**, is that the USA is saturated with illegal immigrants that **ILLEGALLY took their turns, caused the separation of these families, and loss of time and money**.

77. DHS (Department of Homeland Security) estimates the number of **illegal** immigrants in the USA to be close to **11 million**.

78. A respected country would not knowingly allow one citizen to break any law. Now we have a **DISASTER** of 11 million **non-citizens, breaking the law**, for **many** years, **stealing the rights of** legal immigrants, and **demanding** us to **change our laws to make them legal** and our rightful actions illegal.

79. Under Article II of the Constitution, the **President is responsible for the execution and enforcement of the laws** created by Congress, not to make executive orders to suspend the law.

80. The carelessness of the former president in enforcing our laws inflicted ongoing harm upon Plaintiff, his family, legal immigrants, many families of legal immigrants, and society as a whole.

81. The court should **compel Defendants to enforce our immigration** laws.

PRAYER FOR RELIEF

82. WHEREFORE, Plaintiff Tarek Farag prays that the Court:
a. **Declare** that Sharia is contrary to the Constitution and laws of the United States, and should be banned;

b. **Issue an order enjoining** the entrance of Muslims to the U.S. except those who denounce clearly and explicitly without deception, the teachings of Islam that do not comply with our Constitution or laws, and **present their religious books clear from any incompliant, unlawful, or violent teachings**;

c. **Compel** the Defendants to properly vet people entering the U.S.;

d. **Enjoin** Defendants from admitting Elsisi or any other foreign government official that committed violations of freedom of religion into the U.S.;

e. **Compel** Defendants to enforce our immigration laws;

f. **Compensate** the Plaintiff and his family for their damages;

f. **Award** such additional and other relief as this Court deems just.

Respectfully submitted,

Plaintiff: TAREK FARAG, pro se
Date: May 13, 2017

9. EMAILS EXCHANGED BETWEEN PLAINTIFF AND GOVERNMENT LAWYERS

RE: Farag v. Trump - 17 C 2307
Hartzler, Alex (USAILN) <Alex.Hartzler@usdoj.gov>
Mon 5/15/2017, 4:18 PMYou

Mr. Farag,

Per my earlier email, please confirm whether you agree to the following dates:

1. **June 13** (initial status report deadline)
2. **June 19** (initial status hearing)
3. **June 21** (deadline for defendants to respond to the amended complaint)

Thanks.

-Alex

From: TAREK FARAG [mailto:tarekfaragusa@hotmail.com]
Sent: Monday, May 15, 2017 4:06 PM
To: Hartzler, Alex (USAILN) <AHartzler@usa.doj.gov>
Subject: Re: Farag v. Trump - 17 C 2307

Re: Case # 17-cv-2307, Farag vs. Trump

Dear Mr. Hartzler,

Thanks for taking the time out of your busy schedule to discuss with me some of the procedural issues.

As I said to you, and I am not afraid to say it openly, that my complaint is in reality to support the position of our President Donald J. Trump. I hope that the government will not oppose it "just to oppose", or to avoid a court order that looks as if it is against Trump while it is against the order suspending his executive orders.

43

Let me ask you the following questions:

1- Which one is more humiliating to the president; a court order suspending his rightful and constitutional executive orders; or a court order supporting his policies and executive orders?

2- Is the Government going to oppose the facts that I presented to prove that Islamic Sharia is against our laws and Constitution? I am willing and capable of crushing this argument and humiliate whoever tries to do this.

3- Is the Government going to say that Sharia is a good thing and we must apply it?

4- Is the Government going to argue that it has no duty to protect the American people?

5- Is the Government going to refuse to enforce our immigration laws?

6- Is the Government going to say that all Muslims are not terrorists and we must admit anyone who says that he is a Muslim just because he is a Muslim?

I see this case as an unusual excellent opportunity to win it by letting the government agree on the facts and expedite the court orders. We need to notice that the facts I presented in my Amended Complaint meet not only the civil standard of proof (51% to 49%), but also, the criminal standard "beyond a reasonable doubt".

I initiated this case motivated by my patriotism and love for this country that gave me everything I wanted, especially my dignity as a human being, which I could not get in the beautiful country of Egypt, which is destroyed by Islamic terrorists under the watch of those "peaceful Muslims".

I am willing and determined to go all the way in this case knowing that there are real threats to my life, family, and the American people. I assure you that no one paid me a penny, but there are honest people that are helping me with my writing.

Please, accept my kindest regards,

Tarek Farag

From: Hartzler, Alex (USAILN) <Alex.Hartzler@usdoj.gov>
Sent: Monday, May 15, 2017 1:26 PM

To: TAREK FARAG
Subject: Farag v. Trump - 17 C 2307

Mr. Farag,

We've received the amended complaint that you filed this weekend.

Currently, the parties' joint initial status report is due to the court on Thursday, **May 18**; the initial status hearing is scheduled for Thursday, **May 25**; and defendants' response to the complaint is due on Friday, **May 26**.

In light of the amended complaint, we'd like extend those dates to **June 20** (for the initial status report); **June 26** (for the initial status hearing); and **June 27** (for defendants' response to the amended complaint).

Do you agree to the extension? If you agree, I'll file a motion to extend and represent that the motion is unopposed. If you don't agree, I'll file a motion to extend and represent that you oppose the motion.

Thank you.

Alex Hartzler
Assistant United States Attorney
Northern District of Illinois
219 South Dearborn Street, Fifth Floor
Chicago, Illinois 60604
(312) 886-1390
alex.hartzler@usdoj.gov

10. STATUS REPORT

JOINT INITIAL STATUS REPORT

Plaintiff Tark Farag, *pro se*, and defendants, by Joel R. Levin, Acting United States Attorney for the Northern District of Illinois, submit the following joint status report:

A. Nature of the Case

1. Plaintiff Tarek Farag is acting *pro se*. Defendants are represented by Assistant U.S. Attorney Alex Hartzler and by Aaron S. Goldsmith, Senior Litigation Counsel, Office of Immigration Litigation, U.S. Department of Justice.

2. The parties dispute whether federal jurisdiction exists in this case.

Plaintiff's position: Plaintiff argues that federal jurisdiction exist under 28 USC § 1331, the Administrative Procedure Act ("APA"), the Immigration and Nationality Act ("INA"), and other statutes. The Court is authorized to award the requested declaratory, injunctive, and other relief under 28 USC §§ 2201-2202, and the APA, 5 USC § 706. As for the standings of the plaintiff and jurisdictions, this case is very similar to Hawaii CV. NO. 17-00050 DKW-KSC (disputing Trump's Executive Orders banning the admittance of people from certain countries into the USA) with some differences. These differences are that the District Court of Hawaii gave itself the authority to rewrite Trump's order to insert the description "Muslim" in the order, and violated the First Amendment and the U.S. Constitution and Laws by qualifying Muslims to enter the USA in spite of the terrifying teachings of Islam and the acts of Islamic terrorists everywhere. While in this case, Plaintiff's argument is based on undisputed facts about Sharia and the violent teachings of Islam that are against our laws. Our laws do not prohibit religious discrimination in admitting people into the USA 8 USC § 1152(a)(1)(A) "- - *no person shall receive*

46

any preference or priority or be discriminated against in the issuance of an immigrant visa because of the person's race, sex, nationality, place of birth, or place of residence". Islamic ideologies are totalitarian ideologies that are banned already by 8 USC § 1182(a)(3)(D)(i) *"Any immigrant who is or has been a member of or affiliated with the Communist or any other totalitarian party (or subdivision or affiliate thereof), domestic or foreign, is inadmissible"*. Islamic teachings change the mentality and behavior of Muslims to that of terrorists, which are banned by 8 USC § 1182(a)(1)(A)(iii)(I) *"to have a physical or mental disorder and behavior associated with the disorder that may pose, or has posed, a threat to the property, safety, or welfare of the alien or others"*, and 8 USC § 1182 (a)(3)(B)(i)(II) *"a consular officer, the Attorney General, or the Secretary of Homeland Security knows, or has reasonable ground to believe, is engaged in or is likely to engage after entry in any terrorist activity"*. Plaintiff claims that *"The miserable failures of the defendants to protect the country as demonstrated by the attacks of terrorists and losses of lives, made him feel unsafe, terrified, and costing him time and money. For example, when he flies he pays money to the government to torture him in long and time-consuming security lines, and allow strangers to humiliate him and invade his privacy"*. Plaintiff claims that the failure of the government to enforce our immigration laws made his family members lose their opportunity to migrate legally to the USA to illegal immigrants. In spite of the trillions of dollars, our government spends every year from our taxes or collected directly from him and other citizens as fees for security in airports, courts, and other places, it failed miserably in stopping Islamic terror, which are impossible to prevent except by preventing the people that believe in terrorists' ideologies from entering the USA.

The teams of lawyers representing the defendants are violating their duties and the public trust *"Federal employee has a responsibility to the United States Government and its citizens to place loyalty to the Constitution, laws, and ethical principles above private gain"* [https://www.justice.gov/jmd/do-it-right]. They should have been the ones that file such cases and supporting the Plaintiff not opposing him. By trying to dismiss this case, they are:

1) Trying to prove that Islamic Sharia is not against our laws and Constitution;

2) Trying to say that Sharia is a good thing and we must apply it;

3) Committing wrongful acts and carelessly endangering the American people;

4) Declaring that the Government has no duty to protect the American people;

5) Declaring that all Muslims are not terrorists and we must admit anyone who says that he is a Muslim just because he is a Muslim;

6) The Government has no duty to enforce our laws and Constitution;

7) Violating the First Amendment and our Laws by taking actions respecting Islam, hiding its true terrifying nature, and promoting the admission of Muslims that adopt and practice terrorists' ideologies into the USA; and

8) They HAVE NO EXCUSE after the Plaintiff showed the true nature of Islamic teachings SUPPORTED BY THE ORIGINAL ARABIC REFERENCES.

Defendants' position: As a threshold matter, plaintiff has failed to allege any basis for standing because he failed to identify any particularized injury-in-fact which he wants redressed. *See Clapper v. Amnesty Int'l USA*, 133 S.Ct. 1138, 1146 (2013) (explaining that no principle is "more fundamental to the judiciary's proper role in our system of government" than this requirement) (citations and quotations omitted); *Valley Forge Christian College v. Americans United for Separation of Church and States, Inc.*, 454 U.S. 464, 472 (1982) (discussing the importance of this limitation in our system of separated powers). Rather, plaintiff has generalized grievances about how the government operates. *See Lance v. Coffman*, 549 U.S. 437, 439-40 (2007) ("[A] plaintiff raising only a generally available grievance about government – claiming only harm to his and every citizen's interest in proper application of the Constitution and laws, and seeking relief that no more directly and tangibly benefits him than it does the public at large – does not state an Article III case or controversy"). Likewise, to the extent he is challenging potential future action and raising abstract disagreements over administrative policies, his claims are not ripe and should be dismissed. *See Nat'l Park Hospitality Ass'n v.*

Dep't of Interior, 538 U.S. 803, 807-8 (2003) (citing *Abbott Laboratories v. Gardner*, 387 U.S. 136, 148-49 (1967)).

3. Plaintiff states that he is bringing this action "to protect his life, family, property, and community against Islamic terrorists and the failures of the government." Dkt. 21, ¶ 1. His amended complaint lists the following purported causes of action: Count I (Declaratory Relief that Sharia is Incompatible with Our Laws and Constitution, and Should be Banned); Count II (Injunctive Relief Banning the Entrance of Muslims in the U.S. Except Under Certain Conditions); Count III (Compel the Defendants to Vet the People Entering the U.S. to Make Sure They Do Not Endanger Our Wellbeing); Count IV (It Is a Violation of Our Laws to Admit the President of Egypt or Other Foreign Government Officials Who Have Violated Religious Freedom); and Count V (Compel the Defendants to Enforce Our Immigration Laws). Plaintiff asks the court to: (i) declare that Islamic law is contrary to the Constitution and laws of the United States and should be banned; (ii) enjoin the entrance of Muslims into the United States except those who denounce clearly and explicitly without deception, the teachings of Islam that do not comply with our Constitution or laws, and present their religious books clear from any incompliant, unlawful, or violent teachings; (iii) compel the government to vet people entering the country more thoroughly; (iv) enjoin the President of Egypt and other foreign government official that committed violations of freedom of religion from entering the country; (v) compel the government to enforce our immigration laws; (vi) compensate plaintiff and his family; and (vii) award additional relief as the court deems proper. There are no counterclaims.

4. Defendants will file a motion to dismiss.

5. Defendants believe that the principal issues to be decided are: (i) whether the court has jurisdiction over this matter; and (ii) whether plaintiff has even stated a claim. Although plaintiff asserts claims under the Administrative Procedure Act, the APA only provides for review of discrete agency actions set forth in the APA, specifically 5 U.S.C. § 551(13). *See Norton v. Southern Utah Wilderness Alliance*, 542 U.S. 55, 62, 64 (2004) (litigant "cannot seek *wholesale* improvement of this program by court decree, rather

than in the offices of the Department or the halls of Congress, where programmatic improvements are normally made") (emphasis, original quotations, and citations omitted); *Texas Health and Human Services Comm. v. United States*, 193 F. Supp. 3d 733, 741 (N.D. Tex. 2016) (dismissing APA challenge to the resettlement of Syrian refugees). And not only must the agency action be discrete to be subject to judicial review, it also must be *final*. *See id.*; *Home Builders Ass'n of Greater Chicago v. U.S. Army Corps. Eng'rs*, 335 F.3d 607, 614 (7th Cir. 2003). Here, plaintiff has failed to allege any discrete agency action, let alone any final agency for the court to review.

Plaintiff also attempts to state a claim under 8 U.S.C. § 1182, but this provision does not create a private cause of action. *See Alexander v. Sandoval*, 532 U.S. 275, 286 (2001) ("[P]rivate rights of action to enforce federal law must be created by Congress"); *Texas Health*, 193 F. Supp. 3d at 739-740 (holding that the Refugee Act does not create a private cause of action to challenge the resettlement of refugees in this country).

Finally, Plaintiff is not within the zone of interest of any of the statutory provisions he cites, so there is no basis for allowing this lawsuit to move forward. *See Lexmark Int., Inc. v. Static Control Components, Inc.*, 134 S.Ct. 1377, 1389 (2014) (zone-of-interests test forecloses suit by plaintiff whose interests are so marginally related to statute's purpose that it cannot reasonably be assumed Congress authorized plaintiff to sue).

6. Plaintiff advises the court that he has served: (1) US Attorney For Northern Dist. Of Il., Eastern Division, (2) Donald J. Trump, President Of The United States, (3) John Kelly, Secretary Of Homeland Security, (4) Rex Tillerson, U.S. Department Of State, and (5) Attorney General Of The United States, US Department Of Justice.

B. Proceedings to Date

1. Plaintiff filed a "Motion for Declaratory Order Specifying the Elements of an Ideology or a Religion that Should Result in Banning It." Dkt. 14. The court denied the motion

without a hearing. Dkt. 16. Plaintiff later filed a motion to amend his complaint, in which he asked the court to reconsider its denial of the earlier motion. Dkt. 18. The court granted plaintiff's request for leave to amend but declined to reconsider its previous ruling. Dkt. 20. In accordance with this ruling, plaintiff filed an amended complaint on May 13, 2017. Dkt. 21. On May 18, 2017, the court entered a minute order granting the parties until June 20, 2017 to file a joint initial status report and defendants until June 21, 2017 to respond to the amended complaint.

    2.   There are no pending motions.

C. Discovery and Case Plan

    1.   No discovery has occurred.
Plaintiff's position: Plaintiff is planning for discovery.
Defendants' position: No discovery is permitted under the Administrative Procedure Act.

    2.   **Plaintiff's position:** Discovery is likely to encompass electronically stored information.
Defendants' position: Any discovery is not likely to encompass electronically stored information.

    3.   **Plaintiff's position:** No discovery is scheduled at this time.
Defendants' position: Because of the nature of plaintiff's claims and the likelihood that the case will be resolved through motion practice, no discovery schedule is appropriate at this time, and there will not be a trial in this matter.

D. Settlement

    1.   **Plaintiff's position:** Plaintiff discussed settlement with Mr. Hartzler but declined to pursue it.
Defendants' position: The parties have not discussed settlement.

    2.   **Plaintiff's position:** Plaintiff requests a settlement conference.
Defendants' position: Defendants do not request a settlement conference.

E. **Magistrate Judge**

1. The parties do not consent to proceed before a magistrate judge.

2. No matters have been referred to a magistrate judge.

Respectfully submitted,

TAREK FARAG, *Pro se* Plaintiff
****

CHAD A. READLER
Acting Assistant Attorney, General, Civil Division

WILLIAM C. PEACHEY, Director
District Court Section, Office of Immigration Litigation

JEFFREY S. ROBINS, Assistant Director
District Court Section, Office of Immigration Litigation

s/ Aaron S. Goldsmith
AARON S. GOLDSMITH, Senior Litigation Counsel
District Court Section, U.S. Department of Justice
P.O. Box 868, Ben Franklin Station, Washington, D.C. 20044
Telephone: (202) 532-4107
Aaron.Goldsmith@usdoj.gov

JOEL R. LEVIN, Acting United States Attorney

s/ Alex Hartzler
ALEX HARTZLER, Assistant United States Attorney
219 South Dearborn Street, Chicago, Illinois 60604
(312) 886-1390
alex.hartzler@usdoj.gov

Counsel for Defendants

11. MOTION FOR PROTECTION

MOTION TO PROTECT THE PLAINTIFF AND HIS FAMILY

By filing this case, Plaintiff exposed himself and his family to serious threats from the following:
    a) All Islamic terrorists, all Muslims that believe in Sharia, and all Islamic organizations.
    b) Some employees of our government that support or sympathize with Obama and his administration.
    c) The Egyptian government and its agents.

    WHEREFORE, Plaintiff Tarek Farag prays that this Court take the necessary actions to protect him and his family and guarantee his safety, and other relief as this Court deems just.
    Respectfully submitted,

Plaintiff: TAREK FARAG, pro se
Date: July 31, 2017

12. ORDER DENYING PROTECTION

Case: 1:17-cv-02307 Document #: 35 Filed: 08/01/17 Page 1 of 1 PageID #:1155

NOTIFICATION OF DOCKET ENTRY

This docket entry was made by the Clerk on Tuesday, August 1, 2017:

MINUTE entry before the Honorable Gary Feinerman: Motion to protect the Plaintiff and his family [33] is denied. If Plaintiff believes that he and his family are subject to threats to their safety, he should inform the appropriate law enforcement agencies. Motion hearing set for 8/9/2017 [34] is stricken. Mailed notice.(jlj,)

13. SECOND AMENDED COMPLAINT

Note: Attached are the previous 9 exhibits listed in Exhibit 0, and additional 14 exhibits listed in Exhibit 10.
To refer to exhibits, the expression "Please refer to Exhibit 3c page 23" is stated as [E3cp23], and "see Exhibit 2" as [E2].

INTRODUCTION

This case is a civil one, but contains many allegations of criminal activities that need criminal prosecution. As the time goes, Plaintiff discovers new facts, and **expects to discover more facts** especially after running discovery, which **might require him to amend his complaint**. In his civil complaint, Plaintiff seeks the following:
1. A declaratory judgment that **Sharia is incompatible** with our laws and constitution, and must be banned.
2. An injunctive order banning the application of Sharia in any place in the USA and under any circumstances, and ban anyone that believes in Sharia from entering the USA.
3. An order **enjoining Muslims from entering the US,** except those **PEACEFUL MUSLIMS** who **denounce clearly, explicitly, and without deception, the teachings of Islam that do not comply with our Constitution or laws, and PRESENT THEIR RELIGIOUS BOOKS clean from any incompliant, unlawful, or violent teachings**.
4. Compel President Donald Trump to reissue his executive order to better protect the country.
5. An order to compel the defendants to **enforce our immigration laws**.
6. An order to enjoin the government officials from **admitting** the president of Egypt or any other official from other countries that **violates the freedom of religion**.
7. An order to compel the defendants to vet people entering the US to make sure that they do not adopt, practice, or promote a violent

ideology or religion.

8. Compensate plaintiff for destroying his business, which is our nuclear industry. Bill Clinton, Hillary Clinton, Obama, and Obama's administration **destroyed and sold this strategic industry to the Russians for their own benefits**.

9. Protect Plaintiff's life, family, property, and community against the Islamic terrorists or potential terrorists that already entered, or promoting their ideologies in the U.S.

JURISDICTION AND VENUE

10. This Court has Federal Jurisdiction under 28 USC § 1331, the Administrative Procedure Act ("APA"), the Immigration and Nationality Act ("INA"), First Amendment, and other statutes.

11. The Court is authorized to award the requested declaratory, injunctive, and other relief under 28 USC §§ 2201-2202, and the APA, 5 USC § 706.

12. Venue is proper in this District pursuant to 28 USC § 1391.

ARGUMENT

14. This case is very similar to Hawaii CV. NO. 17-00050 DKW-KSC (disputing Trump's Executive Orders banning the admittance of people from certain countries into the USA) [E17], [E18], and [E19]. The Courts' opinions in that case represent a good legal analysis for the issues raised, and the Plaintiff will use them to guide this amended complaint.

15. Tarek Farag is a US Citizen of Egyptian descent and has lived in the US for three decades. Farag **finished his PhD work in Nuclear Engineering** in 1988, while he was in Egypt, and migrated with his family since then to the US. Farag and his wife have four children; they are U.S. citizens and live in different states.

16. Farag is very active in his community supporting the Constitutional and Human rights for all humans. He supports the freedom of religion, especially for Muslims. Farag was unable to go to Egypt to visit his family and friends **fearing** that the Egyptian government could assassinate him. **Farag is living in fear all the time** from assassination by the Egyptian government or an Islamic terrorist.

17. Tarek Farag declares that he sincerely believes in the full equality of humans of different origins, ethnicities, color, religion, or gender within its limitations. He believes in freedoms of religion, speech, expression, and peaceful assembly, to their maximums allowed by the laws and the Constitution of the USA. He further declares that, he believes in the right of Muslims to believe that Islam is a superior religion and all non-Muslims must be killed, however, he believes that no one has the right to harm anyone physically or in any other way, or incite or provoke others to harm anyone even if that one harmed them (it is the role of the law). Farag is an immigrant, and cannot be anti-immigrants; however, he is against anything illegal including the illegal-immigration.

18. Islamic terrorism is completely different from any other terrorism. It is **supported all over the world politically, militarily, and financially by hundreds of billions of dollars**; by **hundreds of millions of individual Muslims, hundreds of Islamic organizations, and tens of Islamic countries**. Even many countries declare that their **Constitutions is based on the ideology of Islamic terrorism**.

19. When people try to neutrally analyze Islamic teachings or Sharia, Muslims rush to wrongfully accuse them of fascism or Islamophobia without knowing the meaning of any of these expressions. For example, Islamophobia is defined as "**unfounded** hostility towards Muslims, and therefore fear or dislike of all or most Muslims" [E1p114]. The fear and dislike of Muslims **is founded** (not unfounded) on the following characteristics of Islam [E1p114]:

    1. Islam is monolithic and cannot adapt to new realities
    2. Islam does not share common values with other major faiths
    3. Islam as a religion is inferior to the West. It is archaic, barbaric, and irrational.
    4. Islam is a religion of violence and supports terrorism.
    5. Islam is a violent political ideology.

Hence, **accusing someone of Islamophobia**, especially after the spread of Islamic terror, is wrong and used to **scare and silence any criticism of Islamic terror**.

21. Sharia law is Islam's legal system. It is derived from the

Quran, Hadith (statements of the prophet Mohammad), and Sera (biography of Mohammad). It is a collection of Islam's teachings and is **mandated** on **every Muslim to follow and apply it everywhere and all the times**. ISIL, ISIS, Boko Haram, Elshabab, DAESH, Moslem Brotherhood, Al Qaeda, and **all Islamic terrorists are the true followers of Islam and Sharia** [E1p99]. Some people give them appealing names like Radical Muslims, or Extremist Muslims. Islam is Islam, there is no such thing as moderate Islam, radical Islam, or cute Islam [E1p100]. We need to **notice the difference between Islam** as an ideology, and **Muslims as humans** that are **no different** from any other humans, but **their behavior can change according to Islam's teachings**. In other words, we **should not have problems with Muslims as humans**, but we **could have problems with Muslims that abandoned their humanity following the violent teachings of Islam**.

22. Defendants have a duty to protect the citizens of the USA from dangerous individuals entering the U.S. with a belief system that gives them the right to kill or terrorize others. They knew and/or should have known, that Sharia (Islamic Sharia Law) is incompatible with our Constitution and laws, and must be banned.

23. Most of the non-Arabic speaking people around the world have the misleading idea that Sharia is limited to how women get dressed or family matters. Islam teaches Muslims how to keep the **superiority of Islam and humiliate and eliminate all non-Muslims**.

24. Professor Hamed Abdel-Samad (a Moslem worked as a scholar in Erfurt and Braunschweig (Germany)), published many important studies about Islam. One of Abdel-Samad's important books is "Islamic Fascism" [E23]. Abdel-Samad concluded from his academic research that: 1) The prophet Mohammad was not a prophet. 2) Quran is not a holy book, was copied from other sources, and many times the copying was done in a distorted way. 3) **Islam is a Fascistic ideology with similarities to the Mafia and Nazism**. [E1p60] [E23].

25. **Sharia teaches the beheading of non-Muslims, expelling them, seizing their property, and taking their women and children as slaves just because they are not Muslims** [E1p72].

26. Sharia orders its followers to hate the non-Muslims and to be brutally violent against them [E1p65], [E3cp118].

28. Islam's ultimate goal is to wage Jihad war against all non-

Muslims to eliminate them until the entire world becomes Islamic [E1p78].

29. Islam practices human sacrifice to please God by killing (beheading) non-Muslims, which is rewarded in life by looting their properties and enslaving their women and children and after death by going to heaven [E1p80].

30. **No freedom of religion in Islam for anyone**, Muslims or non-Muslims, and Islam insults all other religions and criminalizes them [E1p65]. The **death penalty** is enacted for: Muslim men not praying regularly [E3cp36,83,94,131,133]; converts from Islam [E3cp28], [E1p76]; anyone insulting or criticizing Islam or preaching for any religion other than Islam [E1p74], [E3cp28]; **Muslim men capable of jihad and not joining it** [E1p97]; and non-Muslims not paying gizia ("protection tax" to protect non-Muslims from Muslims) [E3cp28].

32. Christians and Jews are allowed to exist in Islamic societies under **very harsh** and **humiliating conditions** to force them to convert to Islam or leave the country. They must **pay the Gizia with humiliation**. They must **follow Sharia**. They **must glorify** Islam, Quran, and the Prophet **Mohammad**, and mention them with blessings. They must not do anything harmful to Muslims, like fighting; not accepting Sharia; or not paying Gizia. They may **not build or repair** their **places of worship even if the Khalifa permitted** them. **Christians should not install bells, towers for bells, visible Crosses, Churches, or have a Church higher than a mosque**. They must **mark** themselves different from Muslims, and when they are naked mixed with naked Muslims (like bathing in public places) they **must put iron or lead rings on their necks**. Muslim workers are forbidden from helping Christians build Churches or make crosses [E3cp**116 to 119**]. All other non-Muslims are considered Koffar (infidels) and must be killed.

33. Islam had peaceful teachings at its start when it had few followers, not enough to use violence to force people to join it. The prophet Mohammad decided to build an army from professional fighters that their only job was to fight to force people to join Islam and increase the wealth of Muslims under the name of Jihad [E1p86]. To justify the looting of the wealth of the non-Muslims, Islam reversed all its peaceful teachings to become very violent against non-Muslims, which Islam considers them improvements and abrogation [E1p65]. Muslims use these conflicting teachings in deceiving their enemies by presenting the peaceful teachings until they feel safe, and then Muslims surprise them with the opposite violent teachings that call for their elimination [E1p88]. At the very least, people will live and deal with Muslims, under the mercy of their whims not knowing which teachings they will apply.

34. **Islam prohibits non-Muslims from imitating Moslems** in their dress, appearance, carrying weapons, riding horses, growing their hair or beard, etc. and **must mark themselves** in a way to **show that they are not Muslims** [E3cp119]. **This is why Muslims insist on Islamic dresses and fight to impose their dress code, especially in foreign countries (like the Burka and Burkini wars), to distinguish themselves from non-Muslims** [E1p42].

35. **Islam applies different rules for non-Muslims to prefer Muslims**. For example, the financial compensation for the wrongful death (Deya) of a free Christian woman is about 16.7% of that for a free Muslim man, and 0% for an atheist man (he should be killed anyway) [E1p61].

36. **Islam mandates its followers to show their superiority and humiliate others** [E3cp118].

38. Islam allows its followers to kill other humans and eat them when they cannot find food, which ISIS is doing in besieged places (they even save them until they need to eat) [E3cp131].

39. Islam interferes with the enforcement of the law and disregards it, and mandates Muslims to act by themselves whenever they feel Sharia rules were violated [E1p65].

40. Islam allows Muslims to use deception to hide their identity and intentions to enforce, spread, and favor Islam, and eliminate other religions (Taqyiah principle) [E1p68]. One example is the **deception of the Grand Imam of Al-Azhar** (Alazhar is the oldest authority in Islamic teachings in the world) when he addressed the German Parliament on March 16, 2016, in an attempt to draw a good picture of Islam in the western countries [E1p118].

41. Islam requires Muslims to follow the prophet Mohammad as the best model [E1p71].

42. Islam does not equate women with men: a) all women are deficient in their brain and religion, and their guile is very great; b) a woman's compensation for wrongful death is half of a man; c) a woman's testimony is half of a man; d) a woman may not be a judge or hold a leading position; e) men are in charge of women and should beat them if they disobeyed them; and f) a man can marry up

to 4 women in addition to unlimited enslaved women from jihad, while women cannot have more than one husband or she must be killed [E1p92].

43. Islam has death punishment for homosexuality [E1p94].

44. Muslims are **using the tolerance of non-Islamic countries to invade** them by immigrants to spread the intolerance of Islam [E1p98]. After the **massacre of Charlie Hebdo** attack, a **huge demonstration of British Muslims** gathered in London **TO CONDEMN THE VICTIMS**, **not to condemn the Islamic terror or the perpetrators of the massacre. They** provided a **petition signed by more than 100,000 British Muslims** calling for the **exceptional respect for Islam** and to **forbid** any one from **criticizing Islam** [E1p135].

45. What we saw and are seeing these days of horrific atrocities by Islamic terrorists are not new inventions of Sharia. Farag and his family lived through many of these applications of Sharia while they were in Egypt. In one incident on May 1981 (the incident was known later as the massacre of Elzawya Elhamra in Cairo). A **Christian man donated his land to build a church, which Muslims consider it outrageously offending to Islam**. Muslims killed the man, took the land to build a mosque on it, and went into horrific killings, lootings, burnings of Christians and their properties **for three consecutive days**. Elsadaat (president of Egypt) instructed the **police to surround the area without doing anything to protect the Christians while helping Muslims in their brutalities**. The result for Christians was more than 80 dead, **more than 20 families burned alive**, hundreds injured, hundreds of homes and businesses looted and destroyed. These numbers could have been much higher except that many Muslim families sheltered and protected many Christians.

46. A draft report from the DHS [E20p21], concluded that citizenship "is unlikely to be a reliable indicator of potential terrorist activity" and that citizens of countries affected by EO1 are "[r]arely [i]mplicated in U.S.-[b]ased [t]errorism." Specifically, the DHS report determined that since the spring of 2011, at least eighty-two individuals were inspired by a foreign terrorist group to carry out or attempt to carry out an attack in the United States. Slightly **more than half were U.S. citizens born in the United States**. The final version of the report, issued five days prior to EO2, concluded **"that most foreign-born, [U.S.]-based violent extremists likely**

radicalized several years after their entry to the United States, [thus] limiting the ability of screening and vetting officials to prevent their entry because of national security concerns" (emphasis added). It is clear from the report that **"Islamic terror" is not closely related to citizenship**, which **leaves Islam as the only factor in terror**. **The most important and dangerous conclusions of the report** are: 1) **more than half of the terrorists were U.S. citizens BORN IN the U.S.**, which means that **they did not integrate in the society,** were **raised in Islam**, and **their terror could happen after more than 18 years**. 2) **Foreign-born Muslims entering the USA BECOME ISLAMIC TERRORISTS AFTER SEVERAL YEARS,** which means that **when we allow Muslim to enter** the USA they do not do terror immediately, but they could **do terror after several years.** 3) **Islamic teachings override all other factors** in the society (like the tolerant environment, freedom of religion and expression, etc.) and **generate Islamic terrorists**. 4) **IT IS IMPOSSIBLE TO GUARANTEE THAT MUSLIMS WOULD NOT BECOME TERRORISTS; EVEN A SMALL PERCENTAGE CAN DEVASTATE THE ENTIRE U.S. AND OTHER COUNTRIES**. 5) **SCREENING MUSLIMS ENTERING THE U.S. IS USELESS IN PREVENTING FUTURE ISLAMIC TERROR; WE SHOULD STOP THEM FROM ENTERING, PREVENT THE SPREAD OF THE TEACHINGS OF ISLAM AND SHARIA, AND DISCLOSE TO PEOPLE THE REAL TEACHINGS OF ISLAM TO RAISE THE AWARENESS ABOUT ITS DANGERS.**

48. Plaintiff voted for Obama on 2008, knowing his Islamic background, thinking that he understands the U.S. Constitution and will follow it. It was one of the happiest days in his life when Obama won the presidency, and was **very proud of the people of the U.S. to allow a minority black person with Islamic background to become president**. This happiness and pride did not last long, they turned to horror as he watched Obama showing complete bias to Islam, blacks, and supporting Islamic terrorists. He ignored completely the mass killings and atrocities against the non-Muslims in Iraq and Syria, and further supported the Islamic terrorists in Syria. This **terrified Plaintiff and subjected him to nightmares being killed with his family by Islamic terrorists**. Plaintiff was **wondering how Obama was able to sleep or go play**

golf with this **horror happening to innocent people under his watch**.

49. General Lloyd Austin, the commander of U.S. Central Command leading the war on ISIS, testified to Congress on 9/16/2015, that out of 54 carefully screened moderate Syrian fighters (to train them to fight ISIS), only 4 or 5 joined the fight and the rest joined ISIS, with a cost of $42 million. **Notice that he does not know the exact number if it is 5, 4, or even 2.139**. This shows clearly the real ratio of Muslims that supports ISIS (if the ratio of moderate Muslims is 30%, then 3% only oppose ISIS, meaning that **97% of Muslims support ISIS**, or even if we assume that 90% of Muslims are moderate, then only 9% oppose ISIS, or 91% of Muslims support ISIS).

50. Plaintiff and his family had lately a friendship with a very nice Egyptian Muslim man and his family. The man is highly educated (PhD in the highest field of research in the human body rejection to implanted organs), lived and worked in France for many years, and considers himself a devote peaceful Sonny Muslim. When asked about the people that criticize Islam, his opinion is that they should be harshly punished because Islam is a holy religion. When asked about the people that convert from Islam, his opinion is that they should be killed because after joining Islam they discovered its secrets and represent danger to Islam. Moreover, when asked about Shia Muslims, he believes that they should be eliminated because they are endangering Islam. This shows the depth of the entrenchment of violence in the brains of Muslims even when they are highly educated and people look at them as very nice people.

51. On August 17, 2017, Muslim terrorists killed 16 people and injured 120 others in Spain. The terrorists were nice looking young men that no one would imagine that they are terrorists.

52. On Sunday August 20, 2017, the police and security forces in the Egyptian village of Elforn, came to arrest and prevent Christians from praying inside one of their homes, because they did not have a permit to pray. **In Egypt, it is a crime for Christians to pray without a permit.** Christians' prayers are offending to Muslims, and result in huge uncontrollable violent rides. It should be noticed that the village has a building used as a church to serve about 300 Christian, but the **security forced locked it to prevent the Christians from praying inside it**.

54. Plaintiff allege that the government was not enforcing our laws;

biased to Muslims; supporting Islamic terrorists; and **bringing Muslims** as refugees without any valid reason, while putting obstacles **against Christian refugees** even when they are continuously **slaughtered by Muslims**. **Farag and his family are living in continuous fear from Islamic terror** inside and outside the U.S. This fear is based on real actions of **Muslims following the true teachings of Islam and Sharia**, not **abstract or theoretical assumptions**. For example, after filing this case and on **April 9, 2017**, three members of Farag's family were praying inside a Church in the city of Tanta (Egypt), while more than fifteen other family members were planning to go inside the church, when a **Muslim detonated himself** inside this Church killing and injuring about 100 Christians. Farag's family members were extremely lucky to suffer minor injuries and not killed. Moreover, to add insult to injury, the Egyptian media showed full sympathy and support to the families of the Muslim terrorists that were compensated huge amounts of money by terrorists' organizations, and ignored the families of the Christian victims, because Islam and Sharia consider Christians infidels that must be killed. Moreover, on **May 26, 2017**, about **ten Egyptian Muslims massacred** and injured more than sixty Coptic Christians visiting a monastery (Farag's family visits monasteries regularly). **Farag believes that a crime committed against a person because of his religion or affiliation with a group, is a crime against each individual member of that religion or group and other similarly situated groups.** Hence, **all the massacres and crimes committed by Muslims** against others, **solely because they are not-Muslims**, are **particularly, personally, individually, literally, and factually** against **Farag**, his family, and **every non-Muslim**.

55. Former president Obama, violated the First Amendment to the United States Constitution by promoting Islam as the Religion of Peace and supported the Islamic terror in Syria and the Middle East with weapons, finances, military training, and political support via our tax dollars.

56. Our security agencies were very negligent and careless in protecting the country from terrorists. For example, the TSA (Transportation Security Administration) treats all citizens as terrorists instead of focusing only on potential terrorists, which is a huge waste of resources and harassment to the citizens. Additionally, when screening people in the airports, they let them go

to **very crowded screening areas packed with hundreds** of passengers **with their bags**, which make it very easy for a terrorist to enter the area with **at least 2 bags full of explosives** enough to **kill hundreds** of innocent people.

57. The US Government and its Agencies **IGNORED the warnings about the Muslim terrorists of the "Boston Marathon"**, and failed miserably to protect the citizens. **In defending Islam, DOJ** (Department of Justice) **insisted that this terror is politically motivated and not an Islamic terror**, which is **outrageously not true**.

58. As if the massacre of the "Boston Marathon" by **Muslims**, was not enough to wake up our government, it **ignored another warning about the "San Bernardino" massacre** by **Muslims**, which again was not enough and **ignored another warning about "Orlando Florida" massacre** by a **Muslim**. I believe that any person can conclude that **these failures are intentional**; considering the billions of dollars spent on all those security agencies, the unlimited resources they have, and their spying power on the US citizens.

59. Upon information from JW (Judicial Watch), the Obama administration was the first in history to dispatch a US Attorney General to personally **reassure Muslims** that the DOJ is dedicated to protecting them [E7], which is a clear bias to Islam.

60. In an unprecedented event, Attorney General Eric Holder assured a San Francisco-based organization (Muslim Advocates) that urges members not to cooperate in federal terrorism investigations that the "us versus them" environment created by the U.S. government, law enforcement agents, and fellow citizens is **"unacceptable and inconsistent with what America is all about"** [E7].

62. JW found that the Obama administration had embarked on a fervent crusade to befriend Muslims by creating a variety of outreach programs at a number of key federal agencies. For instance, **Homeland Security covertly met with a group of extremist Arab, Muslim and Sheikh Organizations to discuss national security matters** and the State Department sent a controversial, **anti-America Imam** (Feisal Abdul Rauf) to the Middle East to foster greater understanding and outreach among Muslim majority communities. The Obama Administration has also hired a special Homeland Security adviser (Mohamed Elibiary) who openly

supports a radical Islamist theologian, renowned jihadist ideologue, and a special Islam envoy that condemns U.S. prosecutions of terrorists as "politically motivated persecutions" and has close ties to radical extremist groups. <u>Obama even ordered the National Aeronautics and Space Administration (NASA) to shift its mission from space exploration to Muslim diplomacy</u> [E7].

63. Former Secretary of State Hillary Clinton allowed the reentry of two radical Islamic academics whose terrorist ties have long banned them from the U.S. [E8].

64. The Obama DOJ threatened that spreading information considered inflammatory against Muslims could constitute a violation of civil rights, which is a violation of First Amendment [E7].

65. The Obama Administration adopted UN resolution 16/18 (an initiative of the Organization of Islamic Cooperation), which limit speech that is viewed as "discriminatory" or which involves the "defamation of religion" specifically that which can be viewed as "incitement to imminent violence". This is a violation of the First Amendment intended to promote Islam [E9].

66. The Federal government is prohibited from involving itself in religion, but the DOJ acted on behalf of Islam in many court cases wasting our resources (e.g. case number 15 C 8628).

67. The Obama administration ignored the **massacres against Christians** and non-Muslims in Iraq and Syria, and **waited until they were decimated**, and then rushed in **pretending** to take action and offered ten thousand Syrians (some claims that they are 200,000) asylums to enter the US. It proved to be an obvious **biased move favoring Muslims**, because the percentage of <u>Christians refugees</u> was less than 1% while their ratio in Syria was about 10% (**1,000% bias** ratio, which indicates an asylum **blockade on Christians**).

68. Obama misrepresented the number of victims of Islamic terrorists stating that the majority are Muslims, which proves again that the **source of this terror is Islam itself**. This fact was obvious from the brutalities and terror between both **Shia and Sunni Muslims** that **share the same ideology**. While the Christian victims were targeted because they were Christians, and they have nowhere to escape.

70. Obama was **promoting Islam** under **interfaith actions;** like prayers, dinners, meetings, services, etc., which is in violation of the

"establishment of religion" clause of the First Amendment, which prohibits aiding one religion or all religions.

71. Judicial Watch announced that it obtained 183 pages of documents from the Department of Homeland Security revealing that the Obama administration scrubbed the law enforcement agency's "Terrorist Screening Database" in order to protect what it considered the civil rights of suspected Islamic terrorist groups. The documents **appear to confirm charges that Obama** administration changes created a massive "hands off" list. Removed data from the terrorist watch list **could have helped prevent the San Bernardino terrorist attack** [E4], [E6].

72. Obama administration officials refused to appear before Congress to explain the decision to purge all references to "Islamic terrorism" and radicalism from public documents [E5].

74. Obama intentionally misrepresented the facts to give the impression that the law-enforcement officers in the whole country are unfairly targeting Blacks and Hispanics, which resulted in the despicable deaths of many officers and will result in more deaths in the future.
[http://www.gopusa.com/obama-lectures-nation-on-racial-disparities-hours-beforeassassination-of-dallas-police-officers/]. Obama (joined by AG Loretta Lynch, Hillary Clinton, and others) induced the perpetrators to be violent against the law enforcement personnel (especially Whites) by saying the following:

> *1. African Americans are 30% more likely than whites to be pulled over. After being pulled over, African Americans and Hispanics are 3 times more likely to be searched.*
> *2. African Americans were shot by police at more than twice the rate of whites.*
> *3. African Americans are arrested at twice the rate of whites.*
> *4. African American defendants are 75% more likely to be charged with offenses carrying mandatory minimums.*
> *5. They receive sentences that are almost 10% longer than comparable whites arrested for the same crime.*
> *6. The African American and Hispanic population (30% of the general population) makes up more than 50% of the incarcerated population.*
> *7. Blacks and Hispanics feel that they are discriminated against, and they are hurt.*

8. All Americans should be very angry for that discrimination.

When examining the statistics on Race and Violent Crime, prepared by Obama's DOJ [http://www.amren.com/news/2015/07/new-doj-statistics-on-race-and-violent-crime/], it will show that during the 2012/2013 period:
> A) Blacks committed an average of 560,600 violent crimes against whites, whereas whites committed only 99,403 such crimes against blacks. This means **blacks were the attackers in 84.9% (5.62 times white's attacks)**.
> B) **Blacks are the attackers 82.5% against Hispanics (4.71** times Hispanic's attacks).
> C) From the figures for the 2013 racial mix of the population (62.2% white, 17.1% Hispanic, 13.2% black), a **Black** is **27 times** more likely to attack a **White** and **8 times** more likely to attack a **Hispanic**. A **Hispanic** is **8 times** more likely to attack a **White**.
> D) The rate of violent crimes per person (relative to whites) is **2.46 for Blacks, 1.255 for Hispanics**.

According to these statistics, Obama mislead the Nation to believe that Blacks and Hispanics are discriminated against, while the truth is the opposite, as follow:
> *1- Obama said that African Americans are 30% more likely than whites to be pulled over*, **while they should be 246% to 562% more likely** (see D and A above). *Obama added that after being pulled over, African Americans and Hispanics are 3 times more likely to be searched*, while searching Blacks should be about **27 times** and Hispanics about **8 times** (see C and D above).
> *2- Obama said that African Americans were shot by police at more than 2 times the rate of whites*, while this shooting should be about **27 times** (see C and D above).
> *3- Obama said that African Americans are arrested at 2 times the rate of whites*, while it should be about **27 times** that rate (see C and D).
> *4- Obama said that African American defendants are 75% more likely to be charged with offenses carrying mandatory minimums*, while it should be **245% to 562%** more likely (see A, D).

68

5- *They receive sentences that are almost **10%** longer than comparable whites arrested for the same crime*, while it should be **245% to 562%** longer (see A, D).

6- *Obama said that Blacks and Hispanics feel that they **are discriminated against, and they are hurt***. **This statement was irresponsible, deceptive, and an open invitation to violence against Whites to stop hurting Blacks and Hispanics**.

7- All Americans should be very angry for the untruthful discrimination presented by Obama, and should demand his prosecution as any citizen committing the same acts.

CAUSES OF ACTION

COUNT I DECLARATORY RELIEF THAT SHARIA IS INCOMPATIBLE WITH OUR LAWS AND CONSTITUTION, AND SHOULD BE BANNED

75. The foregoing ¶1 to ¶74 are realleged and incorporated by reference herein as ¶75.

76. The definition of a religion is "The belief in and worship of a superhuman controlling power, especially a **personal God** or gods". Since Moslems consider Islam, a full system to all aspects of life including religious rituals that are indivisible from the state, hence, **ISLAM IS NOT A RELIGION according to this definition and our Constitution should not protect it as a religion**. Islam is categorized as an ideology that could be protected by the freedom of speech, however, **Islam is a very violent ideology** and our **Constitution does not protect violence, but forbids any kind of violence completely**. Hence, **ISLAM IS CONTRARY TO OUR CONSTITUTION EITHER AS A RELIGION OR AS AN IDEOLOGY**.

77. Challenges to agency actions are reviewed under the standard of the APA, using the legal framework of the violated statute. 5 U.S.C. §§ 701-706. Under the APA, "[a] **person suffering legal wrong** because of agency action, or adversely affected or aggrieved by agency action within the meaning of a relevant statute, is **entitled to judicial review** thereof." 5 U.S.C. § 702.

78. 42 US Code § 2000bb–1 guarantee the free exercise of religion,

with the exception only if the government demonstrates that application of the burden to the person (1) is in furtherance of a compelling governmental interest; and (2) is the least restrictive means - - -.

79. Justice Hugo Black held,
The "establishment of religion" clause of the First Amendment means at least this: Neither a state nor the federal government can set up a church. Neither can pass laws which **aid one religion, aid all religions***, or prefer one religion over another. Neither can force nor influence a person to go to or to remain away from church against his will or force him to profess a belief or disbelief in any religion. No person can be punished for entertaining or professing religious beliefs or disbeliefs, for church attendance or non-attendance. No tax in any amount, large or small, can be levied to support any religious activities or institutions, whatever they may be called, or whatever form they may adopt to teach or practice religion.* **Neither a state nor the Federal Government can, openly or secretly, participate in the affairs of any religious organizations or groups and vice versa**. In the words of Jefferson, the clause against establishment of religion by law was intended to erect "a wall of separation between church and State." Reynolds v. United States, supra, at 164.

80. Various states have "banned Sharia law", or passed some kind of ballot measure that "prohibits the states courts from considering foreign, international or religious law." As of 2014 these include Alabama, Arizona, Kansas, Louisiana, North Carolina, South Dakota and Tennessee [https://en.wikipedia.org/wiki/Ban_on_sharia_law]. In some cities like Michigan there are many people protesting against Sharia and others supporting it.

81. To establish Article III standing, a plaintiff must demonstrate "that it has suffered a concrete and particularized injury that is either actual or imminent, that the injury is fairly traceable to the defendant, and that it is likely that a favorable decision will redress that injury" [E18p9]. The Court stated, *"Dr. Elshikh believes that, as a result of the new Executive Order, he and members of the Mosque* **will not be able to associate as freely with those of other faiths***."* SAC ¶ 90. These injuries are <u>sufficiently personal, concrete, particularized, and actual to confer standing</u> in the Establishment

Clause context" [E17p25]. According to this measure, Plaintiff far exceeded this standing requirement. It is not only in the future that he will not be able to associate as freely with those of other faiths, it is also that he was suffering, is suffering, and will suffer total inability to live normal life, in fear of Muslims that believe in Sharia that mandates them to brutally massacre him and others that never did anything harmful to them even if they helped them (like in San Bernardino's massacre where they slaughtered their coworkers and others).

82- Farag's injuries included financial losses. Examples of these losses: 1) He paid $48 extra fees just for security to file a small claims court case its fees $155. 2) He paid extra $33 on his flight ticket for September 11 Security fees. 3) The government wastes trillions of our tax money on failed and useless security agencies.

83- The government is biased to Islam in violation of both the Constitution and the INA. It denied his family members that are deprived of their human rights the opportunity to get asylum, while giving Muslims the right to get asylum without any valid justification. Additionally, the Christian asylum seekers wait about 5 years to get their cases approved, while those Muslims that Obama brought were given the asylum-benefits immediately. Plaintiff alleges that bringing Muslims as asylum seekers with 1000% bias proves the illegitimate motivation by the Obama and his administration.

84- Plaintiff and his family having to live in a country where the Government has established **Islam as a favored religion**, in spite of its full knowledge of the **terrifying teachings of Islam** that materialized in the devastating massacres by **Islamic terrorists inside and outside the USA**. Farag attests that he, his family, and community, suffer just such injuries here. He declares that the effects of the Obama's Administration bias to Muslims and giving asylum to large number of Muslims **for no reason other than they are Muslims from majority Muslim countries**, are devastating to him, his family, and community, and **resulted in physical injuries** to many innocent people in the USA. Now, no one feels safe, not only in flying, but also, in getting into public places or gathering peacefully.

85. Our societies are established on the natural rule that every one wants to protect his life, enjoy himself, and share their joy with others. Hence, it is **impossible to prevent** a person wanting to kill

himself and others from devastating our country, and deprive people from their right to enjoy their life and share their joy with others. Adding to this, the **complete failure and negligence of our National Security Agencies** from preventing the three Islamic massacres of Boston, San Bernardino, and Florida, after having enough warnings (amounts to **conspiring**).

86. The final two aspects of Article III standing—causation and redressability—are also satisfied. Farag's injuries are traceable to Sharia, negligence of the government, its bias to Muslims, and knowingly ignoring the terrifying teachings of Islam and Sharia. If Plaintiffs prevail, a decision banning Sharia and Muslims would redress these injuries.

88. Plaintiff's claims are ripe for adjudication because they do not rest upon contingent future events that may not occur as anticipated.

89. From the above allegations, there are **real** great dangers from allowing people that believe in **Sharia** to enter the U.S. and commit terrorists' acts that are **impossible to completely stop** or **reverse**.

90. From the above discussion, this Honorable Court should issue a declaratory relief that Sharia is incompatible with our laws and Constitution, and should be banned.

COUNT II INJUNCTIVE RELIEF BANNING THE APPLICATION OF SHARIA IN ALL THE U.S.A.

91. The foregoing ¶1 to ¶90 are realleged and incorporated by reference herein as ¶91.

92. We have areas in the U.S. where Muslims are imposing or try to impose Sharia, while others are banning it or trying to ban it.

93. This Honorable Court should put an end to the disputes about Sharia and enjoin its application in all the USA.

COUNT III INJUNCTIVE RELIEF ENJOINING THE PEOPLE THAT BELIEVE IN SHARIA FROM ENTERING THE U.S.A.

94. The foregoing ¶1 to ¶93 are realleged and incorporated by reference herein as ¶94.

95. There are some people that believe in Sharia, but are not Muslims. Those people are very dangerous to our society and are

potential terrorists. Hence, they should be banned from entering the USA.

96. As the report of the DHS showed and explained in ¶46 above, when Muslims enter the USA, most of the time they do not commit terrorist's acts immediately, they might wait several years or their children might commit terror after they grow up, in a process of implanting seeds of terror and waiting many years to harvest it.

97. <u>**8 U.S. Code § 1182 (3) already does not allow the admission of the people that adopt or promote teachings like Sharia**</u>. It states:

(3) Security and related grounds

(A) In general Any alien who a consular officer or the Attorney General knows, or has reasonable ground to believe, seeks to enter the United States to engage solely, principally, or incidentally in—

    (ii) any other unlawful activity, or

    (iii) any activity a purpose of which is the opposition to, or the control or overthrow of, the Government of the United States **by force, violence, or other unlawful means**, is inadmissible.

(B) Terrorist activities

    (i) In general Any alien who—

        (I) has **engaged in a terrorist activity**;

        (II) a consular officer, the Attorney General, or the Secretary of Homeland Security knows, or has reasonable ground to believe, is engaged in or is **likely to engage after entry in any terrorist activity** (as defined in clause (iv));

        (III) has, under circumstances indicating an **intention to cause death or serious bodily harm, incited terrorist activity**;

        (IV) is a representative (as defined in clause (v)) of—

(aa) a terrorist organization (as defined in clause (vi)); or

(bb) a political, social, or other group that **endorses or espouses terrorist activity**;

      - - - - - -

        (VII) **endorses or espouses terrorist activity or persuades others to endorse or espouse terrorist activity or support a terrorist organization**;

      - - - - -

(D) Immigrant membership in totalitarian party
    (i) In general
    Any immigrant who is or has been a member of or affiliated with the Communist or any other **totalitarian party** (or subdivision or affiliate thereof), domestic or foreign, is inadmissible.

- - - - -

(10) Miscellaneous
    (A) Practicing polygamists
    Any immigrant who is coming to the United States to practice polygamy is inadmissible.

- - - - - - - -

    (D) Unlawful voters
    (i) In general
    Any alien who has voted in violation of any Federal, State, or local constitutional provision, statute, ordinance, or regulation is inadmissible.

- - - - - - - -

98. This Honorable Court should enjoin all the people that believe in Sharia from entering the USA.

COUNT IV   INJUNCTIVE RELIEF ENJOINING MUSLIMS FROM ENTERING THE USA EXCEPT THOSE WHO SATISFY CERTAIN CONDITIONS

99. The foregoing ¶1 to ¶98 are realleged and incorporated by reference herein as ¶99.

101. From the above allegations we can see that Muslims must follow Sharia or get killed, they have no choice not to participate in jihad, they can use deception to hide their intentions, they must discriminate and be violent against non-Muslims, they must commit terrorists' acts, etc., which are all against our laws and Constitution.

103. There are some Muslims that do not believe in the violent teachings of Islam. Since Islam allows its followers to lie and hide their real intentions, **it is impossible to distinguish the peaceful ones from the terrorists**. Hence, we should allow only the entry of Muslims who, not only, **denounce clearly, explicitly, and without deception, the teachings of Islam that do not comply with our**

Constitution or laws, but also, **PRESENT THEIR RELIGIOUS REFERENCES clean from any incompliant, unlawful, or violent teachings, according to which they will behave in our society and raise their children**.

104. The government allowed thousands of Islamic terrorists to enter the U.S. one of whom was the wife of the San Bernardino massacre.

105. Currently, we have fights over Trump's Executive Orders to ban Muslims from entering the U.S. without proper vetting. We have Obama's unconstitutional acts to allow potential Muslim terrorists to enter as refugees.

106. We are a country of immigrants. We welcome and select good people that want to enjoy our values and enrich our society. We are **not a sanctuary for criminals and ideologies that want to destroy us**. **No one has a right to come to the U.S** (except our citizens or to become citizens according to our laws); we give this **privilege** to others that deserve it according to our laws. Hence, no one, including Muslims, **can claim** that he/she was deprived from a right to enter the U.S. when we practice our rights and duties to protect our citizens from any potential harm **however minute**.

108. From the above argument, and watching the real events around the entire world; we should put the safety and the well-being of our citizens first and **ban Muslims from entering the U.S.**, **without owing any apology to anyone**.

109. This Honorable Court should issue an order enjoining Muslims from entering the US, except those PEACEFUL MUSLIMS who meet the previously stated conditions.

COUNT V   COMPEL PRESIDENT DONALD TRUMP TO REISSUE HIS EXECUTIVE ORDER TO BETTER PROTECT THE COUNTRY

110. The foregoing ¶1 to ¶109 are realleged and incorporated by reference herein as ¶110.

111. 8 U.S.C. § 1152(a)(1)(A) does not prohibit religious discrimination in allocation of immigrant visas, but prohibits it based on other factors as stated: "(A) *Except as specifically provided in paragraph (2) and in sections 1101(a)(27) (Definitions), 1151(b)(2)(A)(i) (Immediate relatives), and 1153 (Allocation of* *immigrant visas) of this title, no person shall receive any **preference or priority or be discriminated against** in the issuance of an immigrant visa because of the person's **race, sex, nationality, place of birth, or place of residence**".*

113. From ¶46 above, we found that the country of potential Islamic terrorists has small impact on doing terror, while the teachings of Islam inside or outside the USA is the main motive for terror. Hence, President Trump should modify his executive order to ban Muslims (except those who meet the previously stated conditions) and replace the ban on the six countries by general conditions for any country to avoid discrimination based on nationality.

114. This Honorable Court should issue an order to compel President Donald Trump to modify his last executive order to comply with 8 U.S.C. § 1152(a)(1)(A), and ban Muslims from entering the USA, except those who meet certain conditions.

COUNT VI   COMPEL THE DEFENDANTS TO ENFORCE OUR IMMIGRATION LAWS

115. The foregoing ¶1 to ¶114 are realleged and incorporated by reference herein as ¶115.

116. Plaintiff migrated to the USA about 30 years ago. He waited 10 years to get his turn plus 5 years to become a citizen, to be able to file applications for the immigration of his family members, which allowed these families to migrate after about 15 years from applying.

118. These families' opportunity to migrate came after about 20 years from the immigration of Plaintiff. The parents of these families were nearing retirement age; most of their children passed the age of 21, and could not migrate with their parents. As a result, one family abandoned the migration. The parents only of the second family migrated, but were divided between staying in the USA and visiting their children that most of them had children. The parents of the third family came to the USA with two of their children leaving one, but could not stay as one family and the parents returned with one child leaving one child alone to study and work to support himself.

119. Plaintiff believes that a reason for depriving these families from their legal rights to migrate according to the law, is that the

USA is saturated with illegal immigrants that **ILLEGALLY took their turns, caused the separation of these families, and loss of time and money**.

120. DHS (Department of Homeland Security) estimates the number of **illegal** immigrants in the USA to be close to **11 million**.

121. A respected country would not knowingly allow one citizen to break any law. Now we have a **DISASTER** of 11 million **non-citizens, breaking the law**, for **many years, stealing** the **rights** of legal immigrants, and **demanding** us to **change our laws to make them legal** and our rightful actions illegal.

122. Under Article II of the Constitution, the **President is responsible for the execution and enforcement of the laws** created by Congress, not to make executive orders to suspend the law.

124. The carelessness of the former president in enforcing our laws inflicted ongoing harm upon Plaintiff, his family, legal immigrants, many families of legal immigrants, and the society. It delayed the immigration of the family members, prevented the unification of the members of a family, disturbed the life of all the families, and disturbed the finances of his migrating families.

125. The court should compel Defendants to enforce our immigration laws, allow Farag's families to migrate without separation, and compensate them for their damages.

COUNT VII   COMPEL THE DEFENDANTS TO VET THE PEOPLE ENTERING THE U.S. TO MAKE SURE THAT THEY DO NOT ENDANGER OUR WELLBEING

126. The foregoing ¶1 to ¶125 are realleged and incorporated by reference herein as ¶126.

127. The Obama administration was grossly negligent in admitting people from countries like Haiti without proper vetting, instead of helping them develop their countries.

129. The Obama administration aided the Islamic terrorists in destroying Syria and killing hundreds of thousands of innocent people. When the legitimate Syrian government started defeating them, the Obama administration rushed to bring to the U.S. Muslims only, with very few non-Muslims as a cover-up, without any vetting; endangering our country and in violation of our laws.

130. The Court should stop Defendants from endangering our country, and issue an Order to compel Defendants to properly vet people coming to the U.S.

COUNT VIII   IT IS A VIOLATION OF OUR LAWS TO ADMIT THE PRESIDENT OF EGYPT OR OTHER FOREIGN GOVERNMENT OFFICIALS WHO HAVE VIOLATED RELIGIOUS FREEDOM

131. The foregoing ¶1 to ¶130 are realleged and incorporated by reference herein as ¶131.

132. 8 U.S.C. § 1182(a)(2)(G) renders ineligible for admission "[a]ny alien who, while serving as a foreign government official, was responsible for or directly carried out, any time, particularly severe **violations of religious freedom** . . ."

133. The President might have the power to exclude those inadmissible persons pursuant to 8 U.S.C. § 1182(a)(2)(G), for good reasons. When the law prohibits the admission of an offender but the president excludes him, the president puts him on notice and applies pressure upon him to rectify his actions.

134. It is worth noting that the defendants argued that U.S.C. § 1101(a)(15)(A) excludes those aliens entitled to A-1 visa classification, which is not correct. The provision §1182(a)(2)(G) makes **an alien ineligible** (not an immigrant ineligible), while the provision §1101(a)(15)(A) define the term "immigrant", which states:

(15) The term "immigrant" means every alien except an alien who is within one of the following classes of nonimmigrant aliens—
(A)
>(i) an ambassador, public minister, or career diplomatic or consular officer who has been accredited by a foreign government, recognized de jure by the United States and who is accepted by the President or by the Secretary of State, and the members of the alien's immediate family;
>(ii) upon a basis of reciprocity, other officials and employees who have been accredited by a foreign government recognized de jure by the United States, who are accepted by the Secretary of State, and the members of their immediate families; and

(iii) upon a basis of reciprocity, attendants, servants, personal employees, and members of their immediate families, of the officials and employees who have a nonimmigrant status under (i) and (ii) above;

135. Even if Plaintiff's argument in ¶134 above is invalid, the inadmissibility of the violators of freedom of religion still valid, because we cannot have two conflicting laws.

136. Defendants admitted Elsisi (President of Egypt) around the beginning of April 2017, into the U.S. knowing that he committed grave violations of religious freedom and human rights.

137. Elsisi came to power after his military coupe in Egypt. He formed a team, mostly of extreme Islamists, to enact an Islamic Constitution that discriminates against non-Muslims and declares Egypt an Islamic country, and Islamic Sharia law is the superior law above the Constitution.

138. Elsisi enacted Sharia Law rules that restrict the repairs of Churches or building of new ones, while claiming to give Christians more freedom to do so.

139. Following are some of the sufferings of Christians that Elsisi ignored and/or encouraged:

a) A group of lawyers presented to Elsisi a file containing more than **500 cases of criminal kidnappings** (under the Egyptian code) of Christian **UNDERAGE** girls that were forced to Islam and to **MARRY** Moslems. Elsisi refused to take any action because Sharia Law prohibits these girls from converting from Islam, they now joined the best religion (Islam) and it is in their best interest not to become Infidels. They must stay away from their families **forever** to avoid their pressure, irrespective of **being underage**.

b) In one day, approximately 80 Churches were looted and burned, along with tens of Christian homes and businesses. Up until now, no victim was compensated, and no perpetrator was questioned or arrested in spite of the overwhelming evidence.

c) Three children (ages under 14) were sentenced to 3 years in prison plus huge financial penalty for producing a short video clip mocking ISIS. An Islamic judge considered the video **insulting to Islam because it showed some of its facts**. Moments after calling the case, and without trial, the

Judge ordered their immediate imprisonment without posting bonds (against the rules) and without waiting for the order to be final.

d) On May 20, 2016, in the village of AlKarm (Minya-Egypt), a mob of more than 300 armed Moslems attacked, looted, burned the homes of Christian families, and stripped naked an old woman and paraded her in the street,. The police arrested the five Christian victims and 1 Moslem man, and the victimized families were expelled from the village.

e) In December 2016, an explosion in Cairo Cathedral killed and injured more than 100. Many believe that the security forces orchestrated it to blame Islamic terrorists to show that Elsisi is fighting terror. Elsisi ordered the authorities to close the investigations and the army to repair the Cathedral quickly to **destroy the evidence**.

f) Elsisi pardoned 200 imprisoned terrorists ignoring tens of unjustly jailed Christians.

g) In February 2017, many Christians were brutally killed (burned alive in front of their families) in the city of El Arish (Sinai-Egypt). Both the police and the army **refused to protect Christians**, forcing the expulsion of more than 100 families from the city.

h) On April 9, 2017, Islamic terrorists that were known to the security agencies in Egypt bombed three Churches in the cities of Tanta and Alexandria killing and injuring hundreds of innocent Christians. However, Elsisi (he directs and controls everything including judges, media, elected officials, etc.) never prosecuted the people that organized these massacres or the ones that incited them, and never compensated the victims properly.

140. Elsisi as a military man and a leader of the intelligence apparatus supports Islamic terror, while **playing its card** by pretending to fight it. It is impossible for Trump to rely on Elsisi to fight terrorism, knowing that the Egyptian military is devoting most of its resources to invest in the civilian sector hoping to increase its share in **Egypt's GDP to more than 55%**.

141. **Not exerting pressure on Elsisi to stop his brutal discrimination against Christians in Egypt and his support to Islamic terrorists** is **causing Plaintiff damages.** He is suffering pain due to the brutal religious discrimination against his family

members and all the Christians in Egypt, and the brutality of Islamic terrorists in Egypt and everywhere in the world. He lost his freedom to go to Egypt; and is deprived from his right to visit his family, friends, and the places where he was raised.

142. From the above, it is immoral, useless, and in violation of the law to admit Elsisi to the U.S. The Court should **enjoin Defendants from admitting into the U.S., Elsisi or any foreign government official that violated the freedom of religion**.

COUNT IX   COMPENSATE PLAINTIFF FOR DESTROYING HIS BUSINESS

143. The foregoing ¶1 to ¶142 are realleged and incorporated by reference herein as ¶143.

144. After Plaintiff left his last job with an employer around 2001, he started **establishing his own business in the nuclear field**. He spent many years doing the research to develop a method to separate the isotopes of elements especially uranium for its civilian application, to reduce the cost of uranium fuel for nuclear power stations, to reduce the cost of their generated electricity.

145. Plaintiff succeeded in developing a process and a device to separate the isotopes and applied for a U.S. patent on February 28, 2006 [**E22**].

146. Due to the sensitivity of this patent to our national security, Plaintiff requested the Patent Office (PTO) to keep it secret until a final determination could be made. The PTO refused to impose secrecy on the patent application. Plaintiff sued the government to keep it secret, but failed because the lawyers representing the government were interested in opposing the case, not protecting our national security. After the judge dismissed the case; the parties met outside the courtroom. Plaintiff asked the government lawyer if he could apply for this patent in Iran, since the lawyer is convinced that it has no impact on our national security, the lawyer threatened to arrest the plaintiff if he tried to do so!

147. As the dead time to protect the patent in foreign countries was about one month away, Plaintiff had to file a PCT (Patent Cooperation Treaty) application, which made the application available to anyone in any country.

149. Plaintiff spent hundreds of hours and thousands of dollars to get the patent issued in the USA (9,056,272) **[E22]**, Canada (2674952), and Australia (2007220850).

150. Before and after the patent was issued in the USA on June 16, 2015, Plaintiff tried to market it, but discovered the disastrous fact that we do not have a nuclear industry.

151. Few months ago, Plaintiff discovered that Bill Clinton, Hillary Clinton, Obama, and Obama's administration sold our Nuclear Industry long time ago to Russia, and then destroyed it inside the USA for their own personal gain and the Russian benefit.

152. Exhibit 11 shows details of the development of the "Russian Uranium Deal", claiming that it was for the control of **20%** of all uranium production capacity in the United States, which ended being **90%**.

153. Exhibit 12 shows details of the cash flow in millions of dollars to the Clintons.

155. To kill uranium industries in the USA, Obama's Administration imposed banns on uranium mining in many areas, tried to confiscate uranium-rich lands for Uranium One Inc. (eventually to Russia), subsidized solar-panels, and limited the construction of new nuclear power stations.

156. An investigative reporter, Jon Rappoport, has suggested the Oregon standoff between ranchers and feds, that left one protester dead, could be tied to a Hillary Clinton deal with Russia over uranium mining production [E14]. Weakileaks reported that BLM (Bureau of Land Management) was trying to acquire land in Southern Oregon for Uranium One Inc. to give it to the Russians [E15]. Pete Santilli also claimed that there is circumstantial evidence that Hillary Clinton is involved in the sale of Uranium to Russia [E16].

157. These well-organized actions made most of the nuclear companies struggle and some were bankrupt, as shown from the recent share prices of the following companies: Energy Fuels, Inc. ($1.78); Peninsula Energy ($0.28); Azarga Uranium ($0.24); Anfield Resources ($0.052).

158. A report prepared by EIA (U.S. Energy Information Administration), for "Uranium purchased by COOs (Owners and Operators of U.S. Civilian nuclear power reactors), 1994-2016" [E13], shows details of the annual uranium used and its sources. [https://www.eia.gov/uranium/marketing/pdf/umartableS1afigureS1.

pdf]
Table 1, is part of that report, which shows that the actual **uranium from U.S. sources** was about **6% only** for the years 2014 and 2015. This indicates the **size of the deception involved** in this uranium deal, the **actual share of the U.S. suppliers of uranium is less than 10% not 90%** as the Obama's administration claimed.

Table 1: Uranium used by civilian nuclear power reactors (million pounds U3O8 equivalent)

Year	USA U	Foreign U	Total U	%USA U
2010	3.7	42.9	46.6	7.94
2011	5.2	49.6	54.8	9.49
2012	9.8	47.7	57.5	17.04
2013	9.5	47.9	57.4	16.55
2014	**3.3**	**50**	**53.3**	**6.19**
2015	**3.4**	**53.1**	**56.5**	**6.02**
2016	5.4	45.2	50.6	10.67

159. A report released on June 19, 2017, by the EIA titled "Uranium Marketing Annual Report" [E21], reveals many facts about the U.S. losses due to the destruction of its Nuclear industry. It states:
"The average price paid by the COOs for the **14 million SWU** was **$131** per SWU in 2016, compared with the **2015** average price of **$136.88** per SWU. In **2016**, the U.S.-origin SWU share was 33%, and the **foreign-origin SWU share was 67%**. Russian-origin SWU was 22% of the total, with 18% from the Netherlands, 11% from Germany, and 7% from the United Kingdom" (SWU is the Separative Work Unit, used to measure the work needed to enrich the natural uranium to be able to use it in nuclear reactors).
From this report, we find the following:
14 million SWU x $131 per SWU = **$1,834,000,000**
67% of the cost of SWU = 0.67 x 1,834,000,000 = **$1,228,780,000** (annual losses to the U.S. to enrich the uranium, which does not include the price of the 90% of the uranium from foreign sources). Using Farag's patent, the **$1,834,000,000** cost of enriching the uranium could be less than **$700** million, a saving of **$1,134,000,000** annually, out of which Farag could have made about **$567,000,000** annually as profits, which means that **Farag's annual losses due to**

the Russian-Uranium deal is about $600,000,000.

160. Farag believes that the Russians were able to control large percentage of the uranium industry in Canada, Australia, Kazakhstan, and other countries, hidden under the names of companies owned by the Russians.

161. From the above, this Honorable Court should reward Farag three years of his losses of at least $1,800,000,000,00.

PRAYER FOR RELIEF

82. WHEREFORE, Plaintiff Tarek Farag prays that this Honorable Court:

    I. Declare that Sharia is incompatible and contrary to the Constitution and laws of the United States, and should be banned;

    II. Enjoin the application of Sharia in all the USA;

    III. Enjoin the people that believe in Sharia from entering the USA;

    IV. Issue an order enjoining the entrance of Muslims to the U.S. except those peaceful ones who denounce clearly and explicitly without deception, the teachings of Islam that do not comply with our Constitution or laws, and **present their religious references clean from any incompliant, unlawful, or violent teachings**;

    V. Compel President Donald Trump to reissue his executive order to better protect the country;

    VI. Compel the Defendants to enforce our immigration laws;

    VII. Compel the Defendants to vet the people entering the USA to make sure that they do not endanger our wellbeing;

    VIII. Enjoin Defendants from admitting Elsisi (President of Egypt) or any other foreign government official that committed violations of freedom of religion into the USA;

    IX. Compensate Plaintiff at least $1,800,000,000.00 for destroying his business by the Russian-Uranium deal that destroyed our nuclear industry;

    X. Compensate the Plaintiff and his family for their damages;

    XI. Nullify all the actions of Obama and his administration that were biased to Islam; and

XII. Award such additional and other relief as this Court deems just.

Respectfully submitted,

Plaintiff: TAREK FARAG, pro se
Date: August 28, 2017

14. CERTIFICATION OF PLAINTIFF

I, the plaintiff Tarek Farag, certify under penalty of perjury that my statements in my Second Amended Complaint filed on 8/28/2017, are true and correct to the best of my knowledge.

Plaintiff: TAREK FARAG, pro se
Dated: 9/22/2017

15. DEFENDANTS' MOTION TO DISMISS

Case: 1:17-cv-02307 Document #: 50 Filed: 10/10/17 Page 1 of 3 PageID #:1418

MOTION TO DISMISS SECOND AMENDED COMPLAINT

Defendants Donald Trump, in his official capacity as President of the United States, et al., by their attorneys, move to dismiss this lawsuit under Rule 12(b)(1) for lack of subject matter jurisdiction and under Rule 12(b)(6) for failure to state a claim upon which relief can be granted.

The motion's basis is set forth in the accompanying memorandum of law.

Dated: October 11, 2017

Respectfully submitted,
CHAD A. READLER
Acting Assistant Attorney
General, Civil Division

WILLIAM C. PEACHEY
Director
District Court Section
Office of Immigration Litigation

JEFFREY S. ROBINS
Assistant Director
District Court Section
Office of Immigration Litigation

AARON S. GOLDSMITH
Senior Litigation Counsel

JOEL R. LEVIN
Acting United States Attorney

s/ Alex Hartzler
ALEX HARTZLER
Assistant United States Attorney
219 South Dearborn Street
Chicago, Illinois 60604
(312) 886-1390
alex.hartzler@usdoj.gov

s/ Hans H. Chen
HANS H. CHEN
Senior Litigation Counsel
U.S. Department of Justice, Civil Division
Office of Immigration Litigation
District Court Section
P.O. Box 868, Washington, D.C. 20044
Telephone: (202) 307-4469
Facsimile: (202) 305-7000
hans.h.chen@usdoj.gov

COUNSEL FOR DEFENDANTS

CERTIFICATE OF SERVICE

I hereby certify that on October 11, 2017, I filed the foregoing document with the Clerk of the Court through the Court's ECF system and that on this day, it will be served electronically upon registered participants identified on the Notice of Electronic Filing.

Dated: October 11, 2017   /s/ Hans H. Chen
HANS H. CHEN
Senior Litigation Counsel
United States Department of Justice
Civil Division
Office of Immigration Litigation
District Court Section
COUNSEL FOR DEFENDANTS

16. MEMORANDUM IN SUPPORT OF MOTION TO DISMISS SECOND AMENDED COMPLAINT

Pro se Plaintiff Tarek Farag ("Farag") has now filed his Second Amended Complaint in this action. It has no more merit than his prior two. He still seeks to impose, by judicial decree, far-reaching changes to the enforcement of U.S. law so that it is implemented in a manner more to his liking. After three attempts, it remains clear that Farag's claims lack any basis in law. The Court should, therefore, dismiss this action with prejudice.

Dismissal is required, first, because Farag has failed to allege any basis for Article III standing for Counts I through VIII. He has failed to identify any particularized injury-in-fact that he has suffered in those counts. Rather, he simply has expressed generalized grievances about how the Government operates and raised speculative fears about imagined threats. Likewise, to the extent he is challenging potential future action and raising abstract disagreements over administrative policies, his claims are not ripe and should be dismissed.

In addition, he has failed to state a claim under the Administrative Procedure Act ("APA") because he has failed to identify any agency action, let alone any final agency action, that he wishes to challenge. Moreover, the enforcement of immigration law and conduct of U.S. foreign policy are generally matters of prosecutorial and executive discretion not subject to judicial review under the APA. Although Farag seeks to assert a claim under 8 U.S.C. § 1182 to bar certain foreign leaders from entering the country, that provision does not create a private cause of action. Moreover, it does not say what he thinks it says. His interests are so marginally related to the purposes of the statutes he cites that it cannot reasonably be assumed that Congress authorized him to sue.

Lastly, the Court should dismiss, for lack of subject matter jurisdiction, Farag's new claim that seeks compensation for the alleged damage to his "business in the nuclear field" from alleged deals made by former U.S. presidents and administration officials.

While that claim is meritless, the Court can dismiss it because Farag has failed to exhaust his administrative remedies for that claim, as required by law, and because the Federal Tort Claims Act does not permit challenges to officials' exercise of their discretionary duties.

BACKGROUND

Farag filed his initial complaint in this action on March 27, 2017. ECF No. 1. He filed his First Amended Complaint on May 13, 2017. ECF No. 21. On August 28, 2017, Farag filed his Second Amended Complaint. ECF No. 39.

As before, Farag states that he is bringing this action to safeguard his "life, family, property, and community against the Islamic terrorists or potential terrorists that already entered, or promoting their ideologies in the U.S." 2d Am. Compl. ¶ 9. His Second Amended Complaint lists the following purported causes of action: Count I, "Declaratory Relief that Sharia is Incompatible with Our Laws and Constitution, and Should be Banned"; Count II, "Injunctive Relief Banning the Application of Sharia in the U.S.A."; Count III, "Injunctive Relief Enjoining Entrance of the People That Believe in Sharia from Entering the U.S.A."; Count IV, "Injunctive Relief Enjoining Muslims in the USA Except Those who Satisfy Certain Conditions"; Count V, "Compel President Donald Trump to Reissue His Executive Order to Better Protect the Country"; Count VI, "Compel the Defendants to Enforce Our Immigration Laws"; Count VII, "Compel the Defendants to Vet the People Entering the U.S. to Make Sure They Do Not Endanger Our Wellbeing"; Count VIII, "It Is a Violation of Our Laws to Admit the President of Egypt or Other Foreign Government Officials Who Have Violated Religious Freedom"; and Count IX, "Compensate Plaintiff for Destroying his Business."

ARGUMENTS

I. Counts I through VIII should be dismissed for lack of subject matter jurisdiction because there is no "case" or "controversy" at this time.

Article III of the Constitution limits federal courts' jurisdiction to certain "Cases" and "Controversies." See Clapper v. Amnesty

Int'l USA, 568 U.S. 398 (2013) (explaining that no principle is "more fundamental to the judiciary's proper role in our system of government" than this requirement) (citations and quotations omitted); Valley Forge Christian Coll. v. Ams. United for Separation of Church & State, Inc., 454 U.S. 464, 472 (1982) (discussing the importance of this limitation in our system of separated powers).

Counts I through VIII should be dismissed for lack of subject matter jurisdiction because they raise no actual "case" or "controversy" at this time. For Counts I through VIII, the counts in which Farag complains about the Government's immigration policies, he has failed to identify a particularized injury for purposes of standing and, moreover, any controversy is not yet ripe for judicial review because Farag is asking the Court to address abstract questions.

A. Generalized grievances do not constitute an injury in fact that can be redressed by this Court.

One element of the "case" or "controversy" requirement is that a plaintiff "must establish that they have standing to sue." *Clapper*, 568 U.S. at 408 (citations and quotations omitted). To establish Article III standing, an injury must be "concrete, particularized, and actual or imminent; fairly traceable to the challenged action; and redressable by a favorable ruling." *Id.* at 409 (citations and quotations omitted); see also *Freedom from Religion Found., Inc. v. Lew*, 773 F.3d 815, 819 (7th Cir. 2014) (explaining that "the injury must affect the plaintiff in a personal and individual way") (citations and quotations omitted); *Ass'n of Am. Physicians & Surgeons, Inc. v. Koskinen*, 768 F.3d 640, 642 (7th Cir. 2014) (affirming dismissal for lack of standing where plaintiffs did not "complain about anything done to them personally" by the Government). This principle is a longstanding feature of federal court jurisdiction. See *Massachusetts v. Mellon*, 262 U.S. 447, 488-89 (1923) ("The party who invokes the power [of judicial review] must be able to show not only that the statute is invalid but that he has sustained or is immediately in danger of sustaining some direct injury as the result of its enforcement, and not merely that he suffers in some indefinite way in common with people generally").

In applying this principle, the Supreme Court has consistently held that a plaintiff does not state an Article III case or controversy by raising "only a generally available grievance," claiming "only harm to his and every citizen's interest," and seeking relief that would benefit him no more than it would benefit the public at large. *Lance v. Coffman*, 549 U.S. 437, 439–40 (2007) (citing *Lujan v. Defs. of Wildlife*, 504 U.S. 555, 560–61 (1992)). Thus, the "assertion of a right to a particular kind of Government conduct, which the Government has violated by acting differently, cannot alone satisfy the requirements of Art. III without draining those requirements of meaning." *Valley Forge Christian Coll.*, 454 U.S. at 483.

More specifically to the topic at hand, the Supreme Court has held that private persons "have no judicially cognizable interest in procuring enforcement of immigration laws" in the abstract. *Sure-Tan, Inc. v. N.L.R.B.*, 467 U.S. 883, 897 (1984); *cf. Bilbro v. Haley*, 229 F. Supp. 3d 397, 414, 418 (D.S.C. 2017) (dismissing for lack of standing a lawsuit by a concerned citizen seeking to bar the resettlement of certain refugees on the grounds that it may lead to more crime and the spread of contagious diseases).

Here, to support Counts I to VIII, Farag has made no attempt to identify a particularized injury-in-fact that he claims that he has suffered. He does argue that he has had to pay additional fees in court and to board an airplane. 2d Am. Compl. ¶ 82. But he fails to allege how those extra fees are related to the generalized failure of the federal government to enact the immigration measures he seeks. He also claims that the "the government wastes trillions of our tax money on failed and useless security agencies." *Id.* But any economic impact to Farag himself is "plainly undifferentiated and 'common to all members of the public'" and thus insufficient for him to establish standing. *United States v. Richardson*, 418 U.S. 166, 176–77 (1974) (quoting *Ex parte Levitt*, 302 U.S. 633, 634 (1937)).

Farag's alleged injuries also fail to establish standing because they are speculative. Farag claims that he "was suffering, is suffering, and will suffer total inability to live [a] normal life, in fear of Muslims that believe in Sharia that mandates them to brutally massacre him and others that never did anything harmful to them. . ." 2d Am. Compl. ¶ 81. But Farag's subjective fears about events that are unlikely to ever occur do not establish standing. *Schmidling v. City of Chicago*, 1 F.3d 494, 499 (7th Cir. 1993) ("anticipation, fervor of advocacy, speculation, or even fear is not enough by itself to establish standing"). Farag alleges an interest in protecting the lives of himself, his family, and the community against terrorists, 2d

Am. Compl. ¶ 9, but again, that interest is a textbook example of a generalized "grievance about the government" and how it enforces U.S. law. *See Lance*, 549 U.S. at 439-40.

In addition to failing to allege a lack of particularized, actual injury specific to him, Counts III through VIII should be dismissed because they merely seek "a particular kind of Government conduct," *Valley Forge Christian Coll.*, 454 U.S. at 483, and to "procur[e] enforcement of immigration laws." *Sure-Tam, Inc.*, 467 U.S. at 897. Farag's desire for a particular government policy does not grant him standing to bring those counts of his Second Amended Complaint. *See Valley Forge Christian Coll.*, 454 U.S. at 483; *Sure-Tam, Inc.*, 467 U.S. at 897. Farag apparently feels strongly about the topics in his Second Amended Complaint, but "standing is not measured by the intensity of the litigant's interest or the fervor of his advocacy." *See Valley Forge*, 454 U.S. at 486.

Immigration policy can be controversial. But Farag's disagreement with the Federal Government's exercise of its plenary authority over immigration policy, no matter how heartfelt, does not transform that policy dispute into a case or controversy for purposes of Article III standing. In the absence of a non-speculative, particularized injury, traceable to Government action, and redressable by a favorable ruling, Farag has failed to establish standing, and so Counts I through VIII must be dismissed. *See Clapper*, 568 U.S. at 408-09.

B. **Abstract questions do not constitute a controversy ripe for judicial review**.

"Ripeness is a justiciability doctrine designed to prevent the courts, through avoidance of premature adjudication from entangling themselves in abstract disagreements over administrative policies, and also to protect the agencies from judicial interference until an administrative decision has been formalized and its effects felt in a concrete way by the challenging parties." *Nat'l Park Hospitality Ass'n v. Dep't of Interior, 538 U.S. 803, 807-08 (2003) (quotations omitted) (citing Abbott Labs. v. Gardner, 387 U.S. 136, 148-49 (1967))*. Determining whether administrative action is ripe for judicial review requires courts to evaluate (1) the fitness of the issues for judicial decision and (2) the hardship to the parties of withholding court consideration. *Nat'l Park Hospitality Ass'n*, 538 U.S. at 808 (citing *Abbott Labs.*, 387 U.S. 149).

Here, for Counts I to VIII, Farag has failed to identify any issue fit for a judicial decision or any hardship that he will currently suffer if the Court withholds consideration. For example, he alleges that the Government may in the future admit certain foreign government officials in violation of 8 U.S.C. § 1182. 2d Am. Compl. ¶¶ 134. Putting aside Farag's lack of standing to raise that claim, it is not even properly before the Court because it is premised on future events that may never happen. *See* Minute Entry, ECF No. 16 (denying Farag's motion for declaratory order). That claim, therefore, is not fit for judicial review at this time, and Farag cannot suffer any hardship if the Court withholds consideration. For this additional reason, Counts I through VIII of Farag's Second Amended Complaint should be dismissed for lack of subject matter jurisdiction.

II. **Counts I through VIII should also be dismissed for failure to state a claim.**

Farag fails to state a claim under the APA in Counts I through VIII because he has failed to identify any discrete agency action, let alone any final agency action, that he wishes to challenge. Likewise, he has failed to state a claim under 8 U.S.C. § 1182 because that statute does not create a private cause of action and because, on its face, it does not apply. Moreover, Farag is not within the zone of interests of either the APA or 8 U.S.C. § 1182.

A. **Farag fails to state a claim under the APA.**

The APA provides a general cause of action to "person[s] suffering legal wrong because of agency action, or adversely affected or aggrieved by action within the meaning of a relevant statute." 5 U.S.C. § 702.(1) Under the APA, a federal court can review final agency actions and "hold unlawful and set aside agency action, findings, found to be . . . arbitrary, capricious, an abuse of discretion, or otherwise not in accordance with law" 5 U.S.C. § 706(2)(A).

---

(1) In his Second Amended Complaint, Farag does not specify which purported cause of action is based on which legal theory. However, given that all of his claims relate to government action, it appears that he is contending that each of his claims is based on the APA. To the extent he is arguing that 8 U.S.C. § 1182 creates a separate private cause of action that is the basis for Count VIII, that argument is addressed below in section II.B

This review is limited to the set of discrete agency actions set forth in the APA, specifically 5 U.S.C. § 551(13). *See Norton v. S. Utah Wilderness Alliance*, 542 U.S. 55, 62, 64 (2004) (litigant "cannot seek wholesale improvement of this program by court decree, rather than in the offices of the Department or the halls of Congress, where programmatic improvements are normally made," and instead "must direct its attack against some particular 'agency action' that causes it harm") (emphasis original, quotations and citations omitted); *see, e.g., Texas Health & Human Servs. Comm'n v. United States*, 193 F. Supp. 3d 733, 741 (N.D. Tex. 2016) (dismissing APA challenge to the resettlement of Syrian refugees on the grounds that consultation under the Refugee Act does not constitute "agency action"). In addition, not only must the agency action be discrete to be subject to judicial review, it also must be final. *See id.; Home Builders Ass'n of Greater Chicago v. U.S. Army Corps of Eng'rs,* 335 F.3d 607, 614 (7th Cir. 2003).

Moreover, judicial review under the APA is precluded under 5 U.S.C. § 701(a)(2) when the agency action is "committed to agency discretion by law." *See Heckler v. Chaney*, 470 U.S. 821, 828, 834-35 (1985) (explaining that if there is no meaningful standards defining the limits of agency discretion, there is no law to apply under 5 U.S.C. § 701(a)(2)). The Supreme Court has held that the Immigration and Nationality Act ("INA") confers broad discretion on the Executive Branch, including the decision whether to initiate removal proceedings. See *Arizona v. United States*, 567 U.S. 387, 396 (2012) ("A principal feature of the removal system is the broad discretion exercised by immigration officials. Federal officials, as an initial matter, must decide whether it makes sense to pursue removal at all") (internal citation omitted). Although the Federal courts do have a role in determining whether an alien is inadmissible or may be removed from the United States, that role is limited to the Courts of Appeals reviewing determinations made by the immigration courts and the Board of Immigration Appeals. See 8 U.S.C. §§ 1252(a)(5), (b)(9).

Here, Farag cites the APA as a basis for his claims against the Government. 2d Am. Compl. ¶ 10. However, he fails to allege: (i) a discrete agency action (ii) that is final. Thus, he lacks the two requirements for stating an action under the APA. See *Norton*, 542 U.S. at 62, 64; *Home Builders*, 335 F.3d at 614. Rather his claims are, on their face, broad programmatic challenges to Government policy choices. *See* 2d Am. Compl. ¶¶ 91-109, 115-25 (Counts II, III, IV, VI challenging how the Government administers U.S. immigration law), ¶¶ 110-14 (Count V challenging the President enforcement of immigration law through executive orders), ¶¶ 126-30 (Count VII challenging how the Government "vets" individuals entering the United States), ¶¶ 131-42 (Count VIII challenging the conduct of U.S. foreign policy). In the absence of any final, discrete agency action, his claims should be dismissed.

Moreover, any judicial review would be precluded by 5 U.S.C. § 701(a)(2) because there is no meaningful legal standard for how the Government enforces U.S. immigration law and decides to commence removal proceedings. See Arizona, 132 S. Ct. at 2499. For these reasons, Farag's claims under the APA should be dismissed for failure to state a claim.

As for Count IX's demand for monetary compensation, discussed in more detail below, Farag cannot rely on the APA in support of that claim because the APA by its plain terms does Case: 1:17-cv-02307 Document #: 51 Filed: 10/10/17 not provide for that form of relief. *See Veluchamy v. F.D.I.C.*, 706 F.3d 810, 815 (7th Cir. 2013) ("'An action in a court of the United States seeking relief other than money damages and stating a claim that an agency or an officer or employee thereof acted or failed to act in an official capacity or under color of legal authority shall not be dismissed nor relief therein be denied on the ground that it is against the United States or that the United States is an indispensable party'") (quoting 5 U.S.C. § 702; emphasis in *Veluchamy); Dep't of Army v. Blue Fox, Inc.*, 525 U.S. 255, 260 (1999) (United States has not waived its sovereign immunity when it comes to APA claims seeking money damages). Thus, in the absence of any other legal basis for a claim for money damages – and there is none, *see infra*, section III – a claim for money damages that seeks to rely on the APA must be dismissed.

It is also unclear from the Second Amended Complaint whether Farag is asserting an APA challenge against the President. The President appears to be the subject of Count V, which seeks an order compelling the President to modify an executive order relating to immigration. 2d Am. Compl. ¶ 114. But the Supreme Court has ruled that the President is not an "agency" under the APA and, thus, not subject to judicial review under the APA. Franklin v. Massachusetts, 505 U.S. 718, 796 (1992). And no other authority exists for the Court to order the President to issue an executive order. From the earliest days of the Republic, the Supreme Court has found no basis for the judiciary to compel the President, at the bequest of private litigant, to undertake a particular action that lies in the President's discretion to faithfully execute the law. See Mississippi v. Johnson, 71 U.S. 475, 499 (1866) ("An attempt on the part of the judicial department of the government to enforce the performance of such duties by the President might be justly characterized, in the language of Chief Justice Marshal[l], as 'an absurd and excessive extravagance.'" (quoting Marbury v. Madison, 5 U.S. 137, 170 (1803) (Marshall, C.J.))).

B. **Farag has failed to state a claim under 8 U.S.C. § 1182.**

In Count VIII of his Second Amended Complaint, Farag seeks to preclude the admission of certain foreign leaders by asserting a claim under 8 U.S.C. § 1182(a)(2)(G). 2d Am. Compl. ¶¶ 132-42. This claim fails because this statutory provision does not create a private right of action.

The United States and its agencies are immune from suit absent a waiver of sovereign immunity. See FDIC v. Meyer, 510 U.S. 471, 475 (1994). Such a waiver "cannot be implied but must be unequivocally expressed." See United States v. Mitchell, 445 U.S. 535, 538 (1980). "[P]rivate rights of action to enforce federal law must be created by Congress." Alexander v. Sandoval, 532 U.S. 275, 286 (2001). "The judicial task is to interpret the statute Congress passed to determine whether it displays an intent to create not just a private right but also a private remedy." Id.; see Texas Health, 193 F. Supp. 3d at 739-740 (holding that the Refugee Act does not create a private cause of action to challenge the resettlement of refugees in this country).

Congress knows how to create a private cause of action under the INA when it intends to do so. For example, Congress specifically provided a private cause of action for persons adversely affected by an employer's discriminatory practices based on national origin or citizenship status by allowing private parties to file a charge of discrimination with the Office of the Chief Administrative Hearing Officer. See 8 U.S.C. § 1324b(d)(2). Yet nowhere else in the statute did Congress establish a private cause of action to enforce the immigration laws. In the absence of any kind of "rights-creating language necessary" to "convey a congressional intent to create a cause of action," 8 U.S.C. § 1182 should not be construed as creating a private remedy for an alleged violation. See Texas Health, 193 F. Supp. 3d at 739-740. Thus, Farag's attempt to pursue a claim under 8 U.S.C. § 1182 to potentially bar in the future certain unnamed foreign leaders from entering the country must fail.

Even if Farag could bring a private civil suit against the Government under Section 1182, Count VIII would still fail to state a claim. Under 8 U.S.C. § 1182(a)(2)(G), which Farag cites as the statutory basis for Count VIII, 2d Am. Compl. ¶ 132, "[a]ny alien who, while serving as a foreign government official, was responsible for or directly carried out, any time, particularly severe violations of religious freedom" is inadmissible 8 U.S.C. § 1182(a)(2)(G).(2) A relevant exception exists, however, to this ground of inadmissibility. Individuals who qualify under 8 U.S.C. § 1101(a)(15)(A) for certain visas, including so-called "A-1 visas," are exempt from most grounds of inadmissibility, including the inadmissibility grounds established in Section 1182(a)(2)(G). See 8 U.S.C. § 1102 ("for so long as they continue in the nonimmigrant classes enumerated in this section, the provisions of this chapter relating to ineligibility to receive visas and the removal of aliens shall not be construed to apply to nonimmigrants (1) within the class described in paragraph (15)(A)(i) of section 1101(a) of this title. . .").

A sitting head of state generally qualifies for an A-1 visa. See 8 U.S.C. § 1101(a)(15)(A)(i); 9 Foreign Affairs Manual § 402.3-5(C). Thus, contrary to Farag's assertions, 2d Am. Compl. ¶ 132-33, 8 U.S.C. § 1182(a)(2)(G) is not a proper basis for refusing a visa for an individual who qualifies for a visa under 8 U.S.C. § 1101(a)(15)(A)(i). See H.R. Rep. No. 82-1365, at 34 (1952) (noting "constitutional limitations" that require excluding A visa holders from most grounds of exclusion and deportation); cf. *Zivotofsky ex rel. Zivotofsky v. Kerry*, 135 S. Ct. 2076, 2085 (2015) (noting that

---

(2) The Second Amended Complaint contains a reference to another subsection, 8 U.S.C. § 1182(a)(3). 2d Am. Compl. ¶ 97. That provision bars the admission of certain aliens on security and related grounds. Farag states this subsection also bars "the admission of the people that adopt or promote teachings like Sharia," id., but, in fact, this statutory provision makes no mention of religion or of religious law. If Farag seeks an advisory opinion from the Court on the meaning of 8 U.S.C. § 1182(a)(3) for use in future litigation, this is improper for the reasons discussed in section I.

the Reception Clause "direct[s] the President alone to receive ambassadors").(3) In sum, Farag has failed to state a claim under 8 U.S.C. § 1182.

Farag argues that the inadmissibility bar at 8 U.S.C. 1182(a)(2)(G) still applies to heads of state because the bar refers to "any alien" – not to "an immigrant" – who shall be ineligible for a visa, while 8 U.S.C. § 1101(a)(15)(A) does not address "an alien" but merely defines who is an immigrant. 2d Am. Compl. ¶ 134. Farag is incorrect. As discussed above, the relevant exception to the inadmissibility bar at 8 U.S.C. 1102(a)(2)(G) arises primarily from 8 U.S.C. § 1102, which makes the inadmissibility bar at Section 1182(a)(2)(G) inapplicable to persons defined as non-immigrants by 8 U.S.C. § 1101(a)(15)(A)(i) and (ii). Because 8 U.S.C. § 1101(a)(15)(A)(i) defines certain government officials as non-immigrants, they benefit from the exception at 8 U.S.C. § 1102 to the inadmissibility bar at 8 U.S.C. § 1182(a)(2)(G).

C. Farag is not within the zone of interests of any of the statutes he cites.

Dismissal is also warranted for failure to state a claim because Farag does not fall within the zone of interest of any statutes he sues under. Under the zone of interests test, a plaintiff cannot sue when his or her interests "are so marginally related to or inconsistent with the purposes implicit in the statute that it cannot reasonably be assumed" that Congress has authorized the plaintiff to sue. See Lexmark Int'l, Inc. v. Static Control Components, Inc., 134 S. Ct. 1377, 1389 (2014); see, e.g., Fed. for Am. Immigr. Reform v. Reno, 93 F.3d 897, 902 (D.C. Cir. 1996) (affirming dismissal of challenge to admission of Cuban immigrants and explaining that the "immigration context suggests the comparative improbability of any congressional intent to embrace as suitable challengers" all individuals that consider "themselves as likely to suffer from the

---

(3) As the Attorney General noted over a century and a half ago, the President's right of reception extends to "all possible diplomatic agents which any foreign power may accredit to the United States." Presidential Power Concerning Diplomatic Agents and Staff of the Iranian Mission, 4A Op. O.L.C. 174, 180 (1980) (quotations and citations omitted); cf. United States v. Curtiss-Wright Export Corp., 299 U.S. 304, 320 (1936) (explaining that the President is "the sole organ of the federal government in the field of international relations . . .").

generic negative features of immigration"").

Here, Farag is not within the zone of interests of any of the statutes he cites in his Amended Complaint. There is no indication that Congress intended to authorize him, or other similarly situated individuals, to sue over immigration policy. See Lexmark, 134 S. Ct. at 1389. Any purported injury that he claims from the admission of certain aliens "is an injury common to the entire population, and for that reason seems particularly well-suited for redress in the political rather than the judicial sphere." See Fed. for Am. Immigr. Reform, 93 F.3d at 901. In sum, for this additional reason, Farag's Amended Complaint should be dismissed.

III. Counts IX should be dismissed for lack of subject matter jurisdiction.

Count IX should be dismissed because Farag has not exhausted any administrative remedies, as required for him to sue the United States for damages, and for lack of subject matter jurisdiction. In Count IX, Farag asks for $1.8 billion in damages to "compensate plaintiff for destroying his business." 2d Am. Compl. ¶¶ 143-161. Farag alleges that he spent thousands of dollars developing a patent for separating uranium isotopes to reduce the cost of uranium fuel, but that months ago he discovered that Bill Clinton, Hillary Clinton, and Barack Obama "sold our Nuclear Industry" to Russia and "destroyed it inside the USA," causing Farag to suffer annual losses of $600 million. Id. ¶ 144-159.

The Federal Tort Claims Act allows a person to sue the United States for damages. 28 U.S.C. § 1346(b). But a person cannot sue the United States for damages unless the person "has previously submitted a claim for damages to the offending agency." Smoke Shop, LLC v. United States, 761 F.3d 779, 786 (7th Cir. 2014); 28 U.S.C. § 2675(a) (barring suit against United States for damages "unless the claimant shall have first presented the claim to the appropriate Federal agency"). This administrative claim requirement is a filing prerequisite that cannot be waived. Best Bearings Co. v. United States, 463 F.2d 1177, 1179 (7th Cir. 1972).

Here, Farag does not allege that he ever presented an administrative claim to any federal agency. And because he does not name his alleged offending federal agency, Defendants cannot reasonably search for any such administrative claim. Count IX, therefore, should be dismissed, because it was filed before the exhaustion of administrative remedies, in violation of 28 U.S.C. §

2675(a). McNeil v. United States, 508 U.S. 106, 107, 112 (1993) (affirming dismissal where plaintiff filed suit before exhausting his administrative remedies).

Further, the Federal Tort Claims Act leaves the United States immune from lawsuits challenging officials' exercise of their "discretionary function." 28 U.S.C § 2680(a). That limitation "prevent[s] judicial second-guessing of legislative and administrative decisions grounded in social, economic, and political policy." United States v. Gaubert, 499 U.S. 315, 322 (1991). Farag challenges decisions allegedly made by previous administrations, such as solar panel subsidies and "banns" on uranium mining, that fall within the FTCA's "discretionary function" exception. Alinsky v. United States, 415 F.3d 639, 648 (7th Cir. 2005); 2d Am. Compl. ¶ 155. The Court should, thus, dismiss Count IX for lack of subject matter jurisdiction.

CONCLUSION

WHEREFORE, the Government requests that this action be dismissed with prejudice.

Dated: October 11, 2017

        Respectfully submitted,

        CHAD A. READLER
        Acting Assistant Attorney
        General, Civil Division

        WILLIAM C. PEACHEY
        Director
        District Court Section
        Office of Immigration Litigation

        JEFFREY S. ROBINS
        Assistant Director
        District Court Section
        Office of Immigration Litigation

        AARON S. GOLDSMITH

Senior Litigation Counsel

JOEL R. LEVIN
Acting United States Attorney

s/ Alex Hartzler
ALEX HARTZLER
Assistant United States Attorney
219 South Dearborn Street
Chicago, Illinois 60604
(312) 886-1390
alex.hartzler@usdoj.gov

s/ Hans H. Chen
HANS H. CHEN
Senior Litigation Counsel
U.S. Department of Justice, Civil Division
Office of Immigration Litigation
District Court Section
P.O. Box 868, Washington, D.C. 20044
Telephone: (202) 307-4469
Facsimile: (202) 305-7000
hans.h.chen@usdoj.gov

COUNSEL FOR DEFENDANTS

17. MOTION FOR LEAVE TO RESPOND TO DEFENDANTS MOTION

Case: 1:17-cv-02307 Document #: 53 Filed: 10/11/17 Page 1 of 1 PageID #:1441

On 10/10/2017, the Defendants filed their motion to dismiss, for which the Plaintiff needs until 11/15/2017 to respond, and to schedule a Court hearing on 11/22/2017.

WHEREFORE, Plaintiff Tarek Farag prays that the Court grant him a leave until 11/15/2017 to amend his complaint, set a status hearing on 11/22/2017, and award such additional and other relief as this Court deems just.

      Respectfully submitted,

Plaintiff: TAREK FARAG, pro se
Date: October 11, 2017

18. ORDER GRANTING MOTION FOR LEAVE TO RESPOND

Case: 1:17-cv-02307 Document #: 57 Filed: 10/13/17 Page 1 of 1 PageID #:1445

NOTIFICATION OF DOCKET ENTRY

This docket entry was made by the Clerk on Friday, October 13, 2017:

MINUTE entry before the Honorable Gary Feinerman:Motion for leave to respond to Defendants' motion [53] is granted. Defendants' motion to dismiss for lack of jurisdiction [50] is entered and continued. Plaintiff shall respond to Defendants' motion to
dismiss [50] by 11/15/2017; reply due by 12/4/2017. Status hearing set for 10/17/2017 [45] is stricken and re−set for 12/13/2017 at 9:00 a.m. Motion hearing set for 10/17/2017 [52] and [56] are stricken.Mailed notice.(jlj,)

19. MOTION TO STRIKE DEFENDANTS' MOTION TO DISMISS

1- The first paragraph of Defendants' "Memorandum in Support of Motion to Dismiss Second Amended Compliant" [hereinafter Memorandum], **demonstrates the extent of the disastrous way our government is operating**. The Government, especially the **Department of Justice** [DOJ] (that should apply our laws and Constitution and protect the U.S. citizens) **consider the request of a citizen to enforce our laws and Constitution as they were enacted** (as all law abiding citizens **like**) to **achieve justice and protect the citizens** an **outrageous demand**. Defendants' lawyers admit that they do not care about enforcing our laws by saying "He still seeks to impose, by judicial decree, **far-reaching changes to the enforcement of U.S. law so that it is implemented in a manner more to his liking**". Instead of supporting Plaintiff's requests, they devote all possible resources and a large number of attorneys to fight him, disregarding their job duties towards the country.

2- Plaintiff filed his Second Amended Complaint [hereinafter Complaint] in more than 130 numbered paragraphs, while Defendants filed their Memorandum without numbering it into paragraphs, and without stating Plaintiff's corresponding paragraphs, or stating a concise summary of each paragraph. This violates Local Rule 10.1, which states "Responsive pleadings shall be made in numbered paragraphs each corresponding to and stating a concise summary of the paragraph to which it is directed."

3- Defendants' Memorandum did not discuss with particularity any of Plaintiff's statements and made useless general statements in violation of Rule 7(b)(B). Excluding the repetition of Plaintiff's counts, the 17 pages Memorandum mentioned very few times Plaintiff's statements.

4- All the legal analysis in the Memorandum were presented in full details in the Courts' documents of the most similar recent cases, which Plaintiff presented in his Complaint and attached as Exhibits 17, 18, 19, and 20. Repeating the analysis in the Memorandum without showing precisely and particularly the errors or deficiencies in Plaintiff's statements is done in bad faith to waste time.

5- Defendants' pleadings should be stricken because they are irresponsive, as demonstrated by the following examples from the statements of the Memorandum:

> In page 3: "Counts I through VIII should be dismissed for lack of subject matter jurisdiction because they raise no actual "case" or "controversy" at this time. For Counts I through VIII, the counts in which Farag complains about the Government's immigration policies, he has failed to identify a particularized injury for purposes of standing and, moreover, any controversy is not yet ripe for judicial review because Farag is asking the Court to address abstract questions".
>
> In page 5: "Farag's subjective fears about events that are unlikely to ever occur do not establish standing".

In spite of Plaintiff's extensive arguments showing that the controversies are real and happening now and will continue to happen in the future, the numerous statements of Plaintiff's losses, and the large number of daily atrocities committed by Islamic terrorists all over the world, the Memorandum takes the Complaint's eight counts together as wholesale without any particular showings, and states that Plaintiff and others did not suffer any injury, will never suffer from Islamic terror, has no standing, the controversy is not ripe, and he is asking the Court to address abstract questions. This is the proof of the carelessness of our government, which asserts Plaintiff's suspicions that our government is conspiring with terrorists as expressed in the Complaint. The government wants to wait until further thousands of people are killed, and then, it will still say the same arguments that it is not ripe, it is abstract, these killings does not represent Islam or Sharia, no one will be killed, etc.

6- An example of the frivolous argument of Defendants is the misrepresentation of the statements of the cited reference [United States v. Richardson, 418 U.S. 166, 176–77 (1974)] to deprive

Plaintiff from the right to take action because every one is suffering. They state "- - any economic impact to Farag himself is "plainly undifferentiated and 'common to all members of the public" and thus insufficient for him to establish standing". While the same reference states "[S]tanding is not to be denied simply because many people suffer the same injury." Id. at 412 U. S. 687".

7- Defendants' lawyers failed to argue against many important statements of the Complaint especially ¶76 arguing that Islam is not a religion, ¶46 analyzing the government's report showing that Islamic terror is related more to Islamic teachings than to a country, ¶57 and ¶58 raising questions about government's complicity with terror, etc.

8- All Plaintiff's allegations are admitted due to Defendants' failure to deny them.

9- Plaintiff did not intend to compel President Trump to issue an executive order, but to allow him to explicitly ban Muslims that adopt ideologies against our Constitution and laws.

10- The lawyers representing the defendants are violating their duties and the public trust "Federal employee has a responsibility to the United States Government and its citizens to place loyalty to the Constitution, laws, and ethical principles above private gain". They should have been the ones that file such cases and support the Plaintiff not opposing him, especially after Plaintiff showed the true nature of Islamic teachings supported by the original Arabic references. By trying to dismiss this case, they are:

1. Supporting Islamic Sharia in spite of its violent teachings and confliction with our laws and Constitution;
2. Support terrorists acts resulting from Sharia's teachings;
3. Carelessly endangering the American people;
4. Declaring that the Government has no duty to protect the American people;
5. Declaring that Muslims abiding with Sharia are not potential terrorists and we must admit anyone who says that he is a Muslim just because he is a Muslim;
6. The Government has no duty to enforce our laws and Constitution; and
7. Violating the First Amendment and our Laws by taking actions respecting Islam, hiding its true terrifying nature, and promoting the admission of Muslims that adopt and practice terrorism into the USA.

11- No reasonable person can deny in good faith Plaintiff's requests to ban violent ideologies and their followers from terrifying our citizens, and to enforce our laws as written in the books.

12- **Plaintiff is not seeking complete ban on Muslims, only Muslims that believe in violence and adopt ideologies against our laws and Constitution**. As Taqyah principle (Muslims hide their intention and deceive non-Muslims to achieve their goals of eliminating all non-Muslims,
{see ¶40 of Complaint, and [E1p65]}), is one of the basic Islamic teachings, **Muslim terrorists can pretend to be very peaceful.** Hence, it is very important to **make absolutely sure that Islamic terrorists will never be allowed to enter the U.S.**

13- From the previous discussion, we find that Defendants' response was presented to cause unnecessary delay, in violation of Rule 11(b).

14- **Plaintiff's Count IX is connecting the puzzle of destroying our nuclear industry**. He alleges that the **ban on uranium mining and subsidizing solar panels, are parts of the full picture of the criminal actions** of Bill Clinton, Hillary Clinton, and Barak Obama. **Destroying our nuclear industry** in return for illegal money, are **not discretionary functions of any of them**. 28 USC § 2680 (a) states in relevant part "Any claim based upon an act or omission of an employee of the Government, **exercising due care**, in the execution of a statute or regulation, - - or based upon the exercise or performance or the failure to exercise or perform a **discretionary function** or duty on the part of a federal agency or an employee of the Government, whether or not the discretion involved be abused". **The law does not give immunity to government officials or any person from prosecution for his/her criminal action (taking bribes) either in office or out of office, and are fully liable for the financial damage they cause.** Plaintiff found out that the **FBI was investigating** bribes, kickbacks and racketeering by the Russian conglomerate's American subsidiary, and the **Attorney General's representative sat on the Committee** on Foreign Investments in the United States [CFIUS], **which approved the Russia- uranium deal**. Plaintiff is hoping to be able to **find more disturbing facts through discovery**.

15- Ironically, the **DOJ and its agencies are the ones supposed to bring this action** and **run the criminal prosecution of the alleged crimes**; however, they are trying to **justify the crimes** that could

destroy our national security and allow terrorists to enter the U.S.

WHEREFORE, Plaintiff Tarek Farag prays that this Honorable Court strike Defendants' motion to dismiss, impose sanctions on the Defendants, grant Plaintiff all the relief requested in his Second Amended Complaint, and grant other relief as this Court deems just.

      Respectfully submitted,

Plaintiff: TAREK FARAG, pro se
Date: October 29, 2017

20. ORDER DENYING PLAINTIFF'S MOTION TO STRIKE DEFENDANTS' MOTION TO DISMISS

Case: 1:17-cv-02307 Document #: 60 Filed: 10/30/17 Page 1 of 1 PageID #:1452

NOTIFICATION OF DOCKET ENTRY

This docket entry was made by the Clerk on Monday, October 30, 2017:

MINUTE entry before the Honorable Gary Feinerman: Motion to strike Defendants' motion to dismiss [58] is denied. Local Rule 10.1 does not apply to Rule 12(b) motion, and Defendants' motion [50] is responsive to Plaintiff's allegations. The briefing schedule [57] on Defendants' motion to dismiss [50] remains in place. Motion hearing set for 11/6/2017 [59] is stricken. Mailed notice.(jlj,)

21. PLAINTIFF'S RESPONSE TO DEFENDANT'S MOTION TO DISMISS HIS SECOND AMENDED COMPLAINT

SUMMARY

1. Defendants are **violating our Constitution and laws** by **challenging Plaintiff's Counts I to IV** and asking the Court to **dismiss them**. The government and its lawyers **cannot defend** or promote Sharia or Islam as a **religion** (even if they argue against the **proof that Islam is not a religion**), because they will be **violating the Establishment Clause of the First Amendment**. Moreover, they **cannot defend** or promote **Sharia or Islam as an Ideology**, or they will be **violating our Constitution, Laws, and their duties towards the Country**. In reality, the **government is doing all these violations as ALLEGED by Plaintiff**.

2. The first paragraph of Defendants' "Motion to Dismiss Second Amended Compliant" in its Memorandum [hereinafter collectively Motion], **demonstrates the extent of the disastrous way our government is operating**. The Government, especially the **Department of Justice** [DOJ] (that should apply our laws and Constitution and protect the U.S. citizens) **consider the request** of a law abiding citizen **to enforce our laws and Constitution (as they were enacted) to achieve justice and protect the Country** an **outrageous demand**. They want to criminalize citizens' demands that **they do not like** and say: "He still seeks to impose, by judicial decree, **far-reaching changes to the enforcement of U.S. law** so that it is implemented in a manner more to his **liking**". Defendants' lawyers **do not like and do not care** about enforcing our laws. Instead of supporting Plaintiff's requests, they devote all possible resources and a large number of attorneys to fight him, **disregarding their duties towards the country**.

3. Defendants' motion to dismiss is arguing that: (1) Plaintiff **did**

not suffer any injury; (2) All our **Government Agencies are doing the greatest jobs**; (3) Congress **did not authorize** Plaintiff **to sue**; (4) **Plaintiff is hallucinating** that there are **dangers from Islamic terror**; and (5) The terrorists **did not kill and injure enough people** to make his case ripe.

4. Dismissing a cause of action (Count) is a drastic action that should not happen unless it is clear that the allegations of the complaint, when viewed in a light most favorable to the plaintiff, are insufficient to state a cause of action upon which relief can be granted. Cases are not to be tried at the pleadings stage, so a claimant need only show a possibility of recovery, not an absolute right to recovery. Platson v. NSM America, Inc., 322 Ill.App.3d 138, 143, 748 N.E.2d 1278, 1284 (2d Dist. 2001).

5. Defendants' Motion should be denied for failure to state in particularity the deficiencies in Plaintiff's pleadings, did not challenge any of Plaintiff's allegations of facts, and did not meet their burden of proof, especially when viewed in a light most favorable to the plaintiff.

ARGUMENT

6. The Motion states in page 3: *"Counts I through VIII should be dismissed - - because they raise no actual "case" or "controversy" at this time. For - - the counts in which Farag complains about the Government's immigration policies, he has failed to identify a particularized injury for purposes of standing and, moreover, any controversy is not yet ripe for judicial review because Farag is asking the Court to address abstract questions"*. And in page 5: *"Farag's subjective fears about events that are unlikely to ever occur do not establish standing"*.

Plaintiff is **not complaining about immigration policies**, he is complaining about **NOT APPLYING OUR LAWS**,

Plaintiff injuries resulting from not enforcing our immigration laws are due to: 1) The large number of illegal immigrants that delayed the immigration of his families, caused the separation of those families, and loss of time and money (¶118, ¶119); 2) Blocking asylum to non-Muslims (¶67); 3) Bias to Islam and bringing large number of Muslims (¶67); 4) Terrorists' acts; and 5) Allowing Muslims that believe in Sharia to enter the U.S. (¶45, ¶54, ¶81, ¶82,

¶84, ¶85). All these injuries (controversies) are real and happening now and will continue to happen in the future. In spite of all these injuries and the large number of daily atrocities committed by Islamic terrorists all over the world, the Motion argue that Plaintiff and others did not suffer any injury, will never suffer from Islamic terror, has no standing, the controversy is not ripe, and he is asking the Court to address abstract questions. **Unfortunately, and ironically, while the government was wasting time defending Sharia and Islamic terror; and attacking Plaintiff, two more major Islamic terror attacks devastated the U.S. in the last few days.** On October 1, 2017, at least **58 people were killed and almost 500 were injured** after a gunman opened fire at innocent people enjoying a music festival in Las Vegas, in a **well planned and executed** manner. The Islamic terrorists of **ISIS declared responsibility about the attack, but our government is defending ISIS trying to prove that ISIS is not responsible** to avoid embarrassment, hide the government's own responsibility, and avoid the prosecution of all the officials that allowed this to happen. And on October 31, 2017, **8 people were killed and about a dozen injured**, in an **Islamic terrorist attack** in New York City, on innocent people having fun. The devastating facts about the NYC attack is that the authorities knew about the intentions of the terrorist, many people drew the attention to the terrorist, he had been on the radar of federal authorities, and they **allowed him to do a rehearsal** to his Islamic terror **to perfect it**. The worst part is the statements by three officials **confirming** that the terrorist was **not investigated for potential terror**, and they **do not know why he was on the radar**.

*"Three officials said he had come to their attention as a result of an **unrelated investigation**, but **it was not clear** whether that was because he was a friend, an associate or a family member of someone under scrutiny or because he had been the focus of an investigation"*.
https://www.nytimes.com/2017/10/31/nyregion/sayfullo-saipov-manhattan-truck-attack.html

Plaintiff believes that a normal jury can conclude that the NYC attack, after the other three Islamic massacres (Boston, San Bernardino, and Florida) that the authorities **were warned** about them all, moved the government and its lawyers from being **complicit to being conspiring** with Islamic terror. Amazingly, no one resigned or prosecuted up until now. This is another proof of the carelessness of our government, lack of responsibilities, bias to Islam, and absence of applying our laws, which asserts Plaintiff's suspicions that there are high ranking officials in our government conspiring with terrorists. The **government and its lawyers** want to **wait until additional thousands of people are killed and injured**, and then, they will still say the same arguments that it is not ripe, it is abstract, those killings do not represent Islam or Sharia, no one will be killed, etc. However, the **Court should not wait** any more and take an urgent action to fulfill its **responsibility to the Constitution and Law, the Country, and the History**.

7. The NYC attack shows how wrong and careless the government and its lawyers are. We have Islamic terrorists **killing** people just because they are **not Muslims** and **those who criticize** Islam, however, the government **lawyers fail to realize the imminent and real dangers** to Plaintiff who is **challenging** all the following: (1) The validity of Islamic **Sharia**; (2) The admittance of **non-peaceful Muslims**; (3) The **president of Egypt** who is an Islamic terrorist and dictator that would not hesitate to **assassinate** anyone opposing him; (4) The former president of the U.S. and his administration for their **corruption, bias to Islam, and aiding terrorists**; and (5) The U.S. government for continuing the destructive actions of the pervious one and its refusal to enforce our laws and Constitution. Plaintiff and all rational citizens should feel unsafe and scared. Accordingly, Plaintiff asked the Court and Authorities for protection.

8. It is worth noting the complete failure of our government to prevent the terror attack in Texas in which 27 died and 30 injured. We must not use such non-Islamic terror to justify Islamic terror, they are both terror. As stated in ¶18, Islamic terrorism is completely different from any other terrorism. It is **supported all over the world politically, militarily, and financially by hundreds of billions of dollars**; by **hundreds of millions of individual Muslims, hundreds of Islamic organizations, and tens of Islamic countries**.

9. Defendants' claims that **enforcing our laws is not ripe and is abstract,** show clearly the **deliberate refusal** of our government to respect our laws and Constitution. At which point in **deteriorating conditions will the government and its lawyers stop ignoring the**

law, and at which point will the controversies be **ripe and not abstract**.

10. Defendants wrongfully cite the Supreme Court holding that private persons *"have no judicially cognizable interest in procuring enforcement of immigration laws"*. *Sure-Tan, Inc. v. N.L.R.B.*, 467 U.S. 883, 897 (1984). This case was before March 1, 2003, after which INS ceased to exist and its functions were transferred to the Department of Homeland Security. It was for an employer retaliating by asking the INS to deport illegal immigrants, which have no danger on the employer, while this case is about preventing known terrorists from entering the U.S. to massacre the maximum number of innocent people. Additionally, this cited case was for the removal of illegal aliens, while this case is for not admitting dangerous people. The other cited case of (Bilbro v. Haley) does not apply because its plaintiff failed to allege injuries to support standing. Even if the cited cases were applicable in this case, they will conflict with the right of access to courts for redress of wrongs, which is an aspect of the First Amendment right to petition the government. **28 USC § 1361** states *"The district courts shall have original jurisdiction of any action in the nature of mandamus **to compel** an officer or employee of the United States or any agency thereof **to perform a duty owed to the plaintiff**"*.

11. Defendants argue that Plaintiff *"- does argue that he has had to pay additional fees - -2d Am. Compl. ¶ 82. But he fails to allege how those extra fees are related to the generalized failure of the federal government to enact the immigration measures he seeks"*. Plaintiff stated that those **extra fees were for extra security.** They are due to the **negligence** of the government to: 1) Investigate potential terrorists in spite of having warnings; 2) Enforce our immigration laws, and 3) **Allow potential terrorists** to enter the country. These carelessnessex **created high security risks**; then **spent money on useless security measures;** and **collected this money directly and particularly from the citizens through taxes and fees**.

Additionally, those extra security measures injured Plaintiff further by wasting his time and torturing him in dangerous security lines (¶ 56, ¶ 58, ¶ 85).

12. Defendants are misrepresenting the statements of the cited reference [United States v. Richardson, 418 U.S. 166, 176–77 (1974)] to deprive Plaintiff from the right to take action because every one is suffering. They state "- - any economic impact to Farag himself is "plainly undifferentiated and 'common to all members of the public" and thus insufficient for him to establish standing", which does not make sence. While the same reference states, "**[S]tanding is not to be denied simply because many people suffer the same injury**." Id. at 412 U. S. 687".

13. Defendants argue that for Count VIII, Plaintiff has no standing and the issue of admitting the president of Egypt (who supports Islamic terror and encourages violent religious discrimination) may never happen. Farag's standing is due to his injury as his families in Egypt are continuously subjected to acts of terror, religious persecution, and killing (in the Church explosion) (¶ 54), all of which are supported by Egypt's president. As for Defendants' claim that the admittance of Egypt's president or other officials that are violating religious freedom, would never happen, they actually came and met President Trump at the beginning of April 2017, after filing this case, and those officials are continuously admitted to the U.S. since then. When the Court issues a ruling declaring that those officials are inadmissible by the law, it puts them on notice to stop their religious persecution.

14. Defendants argue that Plaintiff is **challenging discretionary** actions by government agencies, which is not true; he is **challenging agencies' negligence in applying unambiguous laws**.

15. Defendants admitted the validity of Plaintiff's claims, which are mainly to **enforce our laws**, citing 5 U.S.C. § 706(2)(A) "*hold unlawful and set aside agency action, - - -, an abuse of discretion, or otherwise not in accordance with law*".

16. Congress enacts our laws to be executed and the violators to be prosecuted, and citizens do not need further authorization from Congress to watch the enforcement of our laws.

17. Defendants claim that the Executive Branch, have wide discretion in matters related to immigration, including the decision whether to initiate removal proceedings. In this case, President Trump applied his discretion and is trying to remove and stop illegal immigrants, but many people are opposing and suing him. Plaintiff is supporting Trump's position and hoping that the Court would issue an order to enforce President Trump's position, and put an end to the controversies surrounding his executive orders.

18. Plaintiff **did not intend to compel President Trump** to issue an executive order, but to **allow** him to explicitly ban non-peaceful Muslims and enforce our Constitution and laws.

19. **Peaceful Muslims** with the people that are **not biased to Islam**, admit the fact that Muslims are **prone** to committing terror, and **motivated** to do it by the **teachings of Islam**.

20. **Plaintiff is not seeking complete ban on Muslims, only Muslims that believe in violence and adopt ideologies against our laws and Constitution**. As Taqyah principle is one of the basic Islamic teachings {Muslims hide their intention and deceive non-Muslims to achieve their goals of eliminating all non-Muslims (¶ 40, [E1p65])}, **Muslim terrorists can pretend to be very peaceful and say anything to allow them to enter the U.S. to execute their terror**. Hence, it is very important to **make absolutely sure that Islamic terrorists will never be allowed to enter the U.S.**

21. No reasonable person can deny in good faith Plaintiff's requests to ban violent ideologies and their followers from terrifying our citizens, and to enforce our laws as written on the books.

22. Defendants failed to argue against many important statements of the Complaint especially ¶ 76 arguing that Islam is not a religion, ¶ 46 analyzing the government's report showing that Islamic terror is related more to Islamic teachings than to a country, ¶ 57 and ¶ 58 raising questions about government's complicity with terror, etc.

23. The teams of lawyers representing the defendants are violating their duties and the public trust *"Federal employee has a responsibility to the United States Government and its **citizens** to place loyalty to the Constitution, laws, and ethical principles above private gain"*. Rather than taking action to create a safe environment for the American people, they are opposing the Plaintiff. They seem to forget that the plaintiff is one of the U.S. citizens that **pays for their salaries to protect his constitutional rights even when he is complaining about his government**. By trying to dismiss this case, they are:

1) Trying to prove that Islamic Sharia is not against our laws and Constitution, in spite of its terrifying teachings;

2) Trying to say that Sharia is a good thing and we must apply it;

3) Defending Sharia and Islamic terror, and carelessly endangering the American people;

4) Declaring that the Government has no duty to protect the American people;
5) Declaring that all Muslims are not terrorists and no Muslims could be a potential terrorist, and we must admit anyone who says that he is a Muslim just because he is a Muslim;
6) The Government has no duty to enforce our laws and Constitution;
7) Violating the First Amendment and our Laws by taking actions respecting Islam, hiding its true terrifying nature, and promoting the admission of Muslims that adopt and practice terrorists' ideologies into the USA; and
8) They **have no excuse** after the Plaintiff showed the **true terrifying nature of Islamic teachings** supported by the original Arabic references.

24. Plaintiff's Count IX is connecting the puzzle of destroying our nuclear industry. He alleges that the **ban on uranium mining and subsidizing solar panels, are parts of the full picture of the criminal actions** of Bill Clinton, Hillary Clinton, and Barak Obama. **Destroying our nuclear industry** in return for illegal money, are **not discretionary functions of any of them**. 28 USC § 2680 (a) states in relevant part "Any claim based upon an act or omission of an employee of the Government, **exercising due care**, in the execution of a statute or regulation, - - or based upon the exercise or performance or the failure to exercise or perform a **discretionary function** or duty on the part of a federal agency or an employee of the Government, whether or not the discretion involved be abused". **The law does not give immunity to government officials or any person from prosecution for his/her criminal action (taking bribes) either in office or out of office, and are fully liable for the financial damages they cause.** Plaintiff found out that the **FBI was investigating** bribes, kickbacks and racketeering by the Russian conglomerate's American subsidiary, and the **Attorney General's representative sat on the Committee** on Foreign Investments in the United States [CFIUS], **which approved the Russia- uranium deal**. Plaintiff is hoping to be able to **find more disturbing facts through discovery**.

WHEREFORE, Plaintiff Tarek Farag prays that this Honorable Court would:

a. Urgently Declare that Sharia is contrary to the Constitution and laws of the United States, and should be banned;

b. Urgently Issue an order enjoining the entrance of Muslims to the U.S. except those who denounce clearly and explicitly without deception, the teachings of Islam that do not comply with our Constitution or laws, and **present their religious references clear from any incompliant, unlawful, or violent teachings**;

c. Compel the Defendants to properly vet people entering the U.S.;

d. Enjoin Defendants from admitting Elsisi or any other foreign government official that committed violations of freedom of religion into the U.S.;

e. Compel Defendants to enforce our immigration laws;

f. Compensate the Plaintiff and his family for their damages;

g. Compensate the Plaintiff at least $1,800,000,000 for the destruction of his nuclear business, or in the alternative hold this Count in abeyance to allow him to pursue administrative remedy if required; and

h. Award such additional and other relief as this Court deems just.

Respectfully submitted,

Plaintiff: TAREK FARAG, pro se
Date: November 13, 2017

22. THE GOVERNMENT'S REPLY IN SUPPORT OF ITS MOTION TO DISMISS THE SECOND AMENDED COMPLAINT

In his response, pro se Plaintiff Farag fails to address the Government's legal arguments as to why this case should be dismissed. Rather than repeat those argument here, the Government emphasizes five brief points.

First, the Government argued that this case should be dismissed for lack of subject matter jurisdiction because there is no "case" or "controversy" at this time. See Dkt. 51 at 3-7 (citing, *inter alia, Clapper v. Amnesty Int'l USA*, 568 U.S. 398 (2013)). In his response, Farag continues to be unable to point to any particularized injury that he has suffered. Instead, he references a number of terrorist attacks that have recently occurred. See Dkt. 61 at ¶¶ 6, 8. These attacks simply have no bearing on any issue in this case. There is no doubt that Farag sincerely does not want to see terrorist attacks in the future, but this interest is an "interest that a plaintiff holds in common with society at large [and] is too abstract to constitute an injury in fact and is thus insufficient to confer standing." See George v. Islamic Republic of Iran, 63 F. App'x 917, 918 (7th Cir. April 8, 2003).

Farag bears the burden of showing an injury-in-fact that is "concrete, particularized, and actual or imminent; fairly traceable to the challenged action, and redressable by a favorable ruling." See Dkt. 51 at 4 (citing Clapper, 568 U.S. at 409). Because Farag utterly fails to do so, this action should be dismissed for lack of subject matter jurisdiction. See, e.g., George, 63 F. App'x at 918 (plaintiffs lacked standing because they had "never been victims of terrorist acts" and their alleged injury was "purely speculative" and amounted "to nothing more than a generalized fear of terrorism that is shared by many if not most Americans"); Cohen v. Facebook,

Inc., 252 F. Supp. 3d 140, 151 (E.D.N.Y. 2017) (explaining that "subjective fears cannot confer standing absent a sufficient showing of the risk of future harm").

Farag does allege that, as a result of the Government's purported "negligence" in applying U.S. law, he has to waste his time waiting in "dangerous security lines" and to pay extra taxes and fees for security. Dkt. 61 at ¶ 11. His theory appears to be that if the country were safer, there would be no need for airport security and, thus, he would not have to wait in line when he decides to fly in the future and would be able to pay less in taxes and fees. See id. This type of speculation is wholly inadequate to establish a particularized injury for purposes of Article III standing. See Clapper, 568 U.S. at 1146; see, e.g., George, 63 Fed. App'x. at 918; Arpaio v. Obama, 797 F.3d 11, 19 (D.C. Cir. 2015). Moreover, this purported injury is not traceable to any action or decision that Farag is challenging in this action. See Clapper, 568 U.S. at 413 ("We decline to abandon our usual reluctance to endorse standing theories that rest on speculation about the decisions of independent actors"); Arpaio, 797 F.3d at 22-23 (explaining that the purported injury was too remote to warrant the invocation of Article III). Nor is this purported injury redressable by this Court because, even if the country were safer, there would still be a need for airport security and Farag would still have to wait in line and would still have to pay taxes. See Clapper, 568 U.S. at 409, 413.[1]

---

[1] The only legal analysis that Plaintiff provides regarding standing appears in paragraph 10 of his response. See Dkt. 61. He takes issue with the Government citing Supreme Court authority for the proposition that private persons have no "judicially cognizable interest in procuring enforcement of immigration laws." Id. at ¶ 10 (referencing Sure-Tan, Inc. v. N.L.R.B., 467 U.S. 883, 897 (1984)). Plaintiff argues that this authority is not applicable because it predates the establishment of the Department of Homeland Security ("DHS"). Id. at ¶ 10. But the creation of DHS is irrelevant to the issue of whether a private party has an interest in procuring the enforcement of immigration law. Second, he argues that Sure-Tan is distinguishable from the present case because it involves illegal immigrants rather than terrorists. See id. But Plaintiff never explains why this difference should matter with respect to the question of whether a plaintiff has standing. Third, Plaintiff argues that even if Sure-Tan is applicable, this Court should not apply it because it is in conflict with the First Amendment. Id. Obviously, there is no merit to this contention; if binding Supreme Court precedent is applicable it must be applied by district courts. Plaintiff also argues that Bilbro v. Haley does not apply because in that case the plaintiff failed to allege injuries to support standing. See id. (citing 229 F. Supp. 3d 397, 414

(D.S.C. 2017)). In fact, the alleged injuries in that case – a purported increase in "terrorist activity," crime, and disease allegedly flowing from the admission of refugees – is very similar to the alleged injuries in the case. See Bilbro, 229 F. Supp. 3d at 414. In both cases, the alleged injuries are simply insufficient to establish standing.

Second, the Government argued that any claims that Farag might have are not ripe at this time. See Dkt. 51 at 6-7. Farag fails to respond to this argument at all, other than to state:

> Defendants' claims that enforcing our laws is not ripe and is abstract, show clearly the deliberate refusal of our government to respect our laws and Constitution. At which point in deteriorating conditions will the government and its lawyers stop ignoring the law, and at which point will the controversies be ripe and not abstract.

Dkt. 61 at ¶ 9 (emphasis omitted). It is unclear what this statement even means other than Farag is unhappy that the Government raised this legal argument. In any event, this statement is not responsive to the Government's argument that Farag lacks a ripe claim at this time. See Minute Entry, Dkt. No. 16 (denying Farag's motion for declaratory order).

Third, the Government argued that Farag failed to state a claim under 8 U.S.C. § 1182 and, thus, for this independent reason Count VIII should be dismissed. See Dkt. 51 at 11-13.(2) Farag fails to respond to this legal argument other than to state his opinion that if this Court declared that certain unidentified foreign leaders were barred from entering this country, they would be "on notice to stop their religious persecution." Dkt. 61 at ¶ 13. Because this is not a legal argument and, in any event, is not responsive to the motion to dismiss, this Court may properly treat as uncontested the Government's argument that Count VIII should be dismissed for failure to state a claim. Cf. Steen v. Myers, 486 F.3d 1017, 1020-21 (7th Cir. 2007) (absence of discussion in briefs amounts to abandonment of claim).

---

(2) The Government also noted that the Reception Clause "direct[s] the President alone to receive ambassadors." *See* Dkt. 51 at 12-13 (citing *Zivotofsky ex rel. Zivotofsky v. Kerry*, 135 S. Ct. 2076, 2085 (2015)).

Fourth, Farag clarifies that he is seeking to compel action under 5 U.S.C. § 706(2)(A) of the Administrative Procedure Act ("APA"). Dkt. 61 at ¶ 15. But, as previously noted, this provision of the APA only allows Courts to "set aside" final agency action that is "arbitrary, capricious, an abuse of discretion, or otherwise not in accordance with law." See Dkt. 51 at 8-9 discussing 5 U.S.C. § 706(2)(A). Because Farag is not seeking to vacate or set aside any agency action, this statutory provision does not support any of Farag's claims.

Fifth, in his response, Farag changes his position stating that he is no longer seeking to compel the Executive to issue any orders, but instead is seeking to "allow" the Executive to "enforce our Constitution and laws." Compare Dkt. 61 at ¶ 18 (emphasis omitted) with 2d Am. Compl. ¶ 9, Count V. It is unclear what Farag means by this. Under our Constitution, the Executive already has the authority to enforce the law. See U.S. Const., Art. II, Sec. 1 ("The executive power shall be vested in a President of the United States of America"); see generally, U.S. Const., Art. II, Sec. 3 ("[H]e shall take care that the laws be faithfully executed . . ."). Thus, there is no basis for this Court to enter an order allowing the Executive to enforce the law.

WHEREFORE, for the reasons stated in the Government's motion to dismiss and this reply, this Court should dismiss Farag's second amended complaint with prejudice.

Dated: December 4, 2017   Respectfully submitted,

    CHAD A. READLER
    Principal Deputy Assistant Attorney General
    Civil Division

    WILLIAM C. PEACHEY
    Director
    District Court Section
    Office of Immigration Litigation

    JEFFREY S. ROBINS
    Assistant Director
    District Court Section

Office of Immigration Litigation

HANS H. CHEN
Senior Litigation Counsel
District Court Section
Office of Immigration Litigation

s/ Aaron S. Goldsmith
AARON S. GOLDSMITH
Senior Litigation Counsel
District Court Section
U.S. Department of Justice
P.O. Box 868, Ben Franklin Station
Washington, D.C. 20044
Telephone: (202) 532-4107
Aaron.Goldsmith@usdoj.gov

JOEL R. LEVIN
Acting United States Attorney

ALEX HARTZLER
Assistant United States Attorney
219 South Dearborn Street
Chicago, Illinois 60604
(312) 886-1390
alex.hartzler@usdoj.gov

COUNSEL FOR DEFENDANTS

23. MOTION TO CLARIFY PLAINTIFF'S POSITIONS IN RESPONSE TO GOVERNMENT'S REPLY

Defendants filed their "Reply in Support of its Motion to Dismiss the Second Amended Complaint" scoffing at Plaintiff as if they could not understand what he means or his positions. Hence, Plaintiff is filing this motion to clarify his statements and positions.

1) Defendants were unable to point to any injury-in-fact that is concrete, particularized, and actual or imminent; fairly traceable to the challenged action, and redressable by a favorable ruling that Plaintiff has suffered, in spite of all the injuries he, his family, and millions around the world suffered. It seems that Defendants believe that the **Plaintiff must be killed** in order to **have standing to sue**, and then Defendants can claim that they have **immunity from being sued**.

2) Yes, Plaintiff claims that if the country were safer, there would be no need for extravagant airport security or other useless and very expensive security measures everywhere that all security experts have admitted that it is impossible to prevent a terrorist attack. We need to have **smart security** measures that remove all the potential terrorists from the country or at least fully monitor them.

3) Defendants' lawyers negligently failed miserably to recognize that **Plaintiff and his family were victims of actual terrorists' acts**, while the plaintiffs in the cited case "lacked standing because they had "never been victims of terrorist acts"".

4) Defendants' lawyers could not understand what Plaintiff's ¶9 means, which states:

> "Defendants' claims that **enforcing our laws is not ripe and is abstract**, show clearly the **deliberate refusal** of our government to respect our laws and Constitution. At which point in **deteriorating conditions will the government and its lawyers stop ignoring the**

law, and at which point will the controversies be **ripe** and **not abstract**".

It means that the **Defendants are refusing to enforce our laws that ban potential terrorists** from entering the country **or watch them**, waiting for **another disaster** to happened **in addition to the latest one in New York**, The Defendants will keep saying that **all these disasters** are **not enough for us to take action** (**not ripe**), and they are **just hallucinations** in the minds of sick people and **did not injure anyone** (**abstract).**

    WHEREFORE, Plaintiff Tarek Farag prays that this Honorable Court allow this motion to be included in the pleadings, and grant other relief as this Court deems just.

    Respectfully submitted,

Plaintiff: TAREK FARAG, pro se
Date: December 4, 2017

24. ORDER DEEMING PLAINTIFF'S MOTION TO CLARIFY A SURREPLY

NOTIFICATION OF DOCKET ENTRY

This docket entry was made by the Clerk on Tuesday, December 5, 2017:

MINUTE entry before the Honorable Gary Feinerman: Motion to clarify Plaintiff's positions in response to Government's reply [64] is granted. Plaintiff's motion will be deemed a surreply. Motion hearing set for 12/13/2017 [65] is stricken.Mailed notice. (jlj,)

---

25. ORDER RE-SETTING STATUS HEARING

NOTIFICATION OF DOCKET ENTRY

This docket entry was made by the Clerk on Monday, December 11, 2017:

MINUTE entry before the Honorable Gary Feinerman: Status hearing set for 12/13/2017 at 9:00 a.m. [57] is re–set for 9:15 a.m. TIME CHANGE ONLY.Mailed notice. (jlj,)

26. ORDER GRANTING DEFENDANTS' MOTION TO DISMISS

NOTIFICATION OF DOCKET ENTRY

This docket entry was made by the Clerk on Tuesday, December 12, 2017:

MINUTE entry before the Honorable Gary Feinerman: Defendants' motion to dismiss [50] is granted. Counts I–VIII of the operative complaint [39] are dismissed for lack of subject matter jurisdiction, and Count IX is dismissed without prejudice for failure to exhaust administrative remedies. The 12/13/2017 status hearing [67] is stricken. Enter judgment order. Civil case closed. Mailed notice. (jlj,)

27. COURT ORDER AND OPINION

ORDER

For the reasons set forth below, Defendants' motion to dismiss [50] is granted. Counts I-VIII of the operative complaint [39] are dismissed for lack of subject matter jurisdiction, and Count IX is dismissed without prejudice for failure to exhaust administrative remedies. The 12/13/2017 status hearing [67] is stricken. Enter judgment order. Civil case closed.

STATEMENT

Plaintiff Tarek Farag sues the United States, two of its departments, and three of its executive officials in their official capacities. Docs. 1, 39. The claims against the departments and executive officials are treated as claims against the United States itself, so all Defendants will be referred to collectively as the United States. *See Golub v. United States*, 593 F. App'x 546, 549-50 (7th Cir. 2014); *Del Raine v. Carlson*, 826 F.2d 698, 703 (7th Cir. 1987).

Counts I-VIII of the operative complaint allege that the United States has in several respects failed to enforce the Nation's immigration laws with proper vigor. Farag does not have Article III standing to pursue those claims, which state only general grievances about the conduct of government, and which seek relief that would affect him no more directly than the public at large. *See Lance v. Coffman*, 549 U.S. 437, 439-40 (2007); *Valley Forge Christian Coll. v. Ams. United for Separation of Church & State, Inc.*, 454 U.S. 464, 472, 483 (1982); *Freedom from Religion Found., Inc. v. Lew*, 773 F.3d 815, 819 (7th Cir. 2014). Moreover, as a private citizen, Farag has no Article III standing to seek to procure enforcement of the immigration laws by the federal government. *See Sure-Tan, Inc. v. NLRB*, 467 U.S. 883, 897 (1984).

Count IX of the operative complaint alleges that the United States (through prior executive officials) took action with respect to domestic uranium production that significantly harmed Farag's nuclear energy business. Such a claim, if it exists at all, lies under the Federal Tort Claims Act ("FTCA"), 28 U.S.C. § 1346(b), and a person cannot bring an FTCA claim in court without first exhausting his or her administrative remedies by submitting a claim for damages to the allegedly offending agency. *See Smoke Shop, LLC v. United States*, 761 F.3d 779, 786 (7th Cir. 2014); 28 U.S.C. § 2675(a). The United States asserts that Farag has not presented a claim to any federal agency, and Farag does not dispute that assertion, so Count IX is dismissed without prejudice for failure to exhaust. *See McNeil v. United States*, 508 U.S. 106 (1993).

The operative complaint is Farag's second amended (and thus third overall) complaint. In light of the opportunities he already has been given to state a viable claim, and given the grounds for dismissing his claims, Farag will not be given an opportunity to replead, and judgment will be entered. *See Bank of Am., N.A. v. Knight*, 725 F.3d 815, 818-19 (7th Cir. 2013); *Agnew v. NCAA*, 683 F.3d 328, 347 (7th Cir. 2012).

December 12, 2017

JUDGE GARY FEINERMAN
United States District Judge

28. MOTION TO RECONSIDER THE COURT ORDER DISMISSING THE COMPLAINT

1) On 12/12/17, the Court dismissed Count IX of the complaint [39] without prejudice for failure to exhaust administrative remedies, and Counts I-VIII for lack of subject matter jurisdiction, because "*Farag does not have Article III standing to pursue those claims, which state only **general grievances** about the conduct of government, and which **seek relief that would affect him no more directly than the public at large***".

2) The Court overlooked that ("*The party who invokes the [judicial] power must be able to show ... that he has sustained or is immediately in danger of sustaining some direct injury ... and not merely that he suffers in some indefinite way in common with people generally.*") [Massachusetts v. Mellon, 262 U.S. 447, 488, 43 S.Ct. 597, 67 L.Ed. 1078 (1923)]. As for Counts I to IV, **if the Court would not accept,** as enough **injuries** to give Plaintiff standing, **his dreadful situations, the adherents of Sharia subjected him and his family to** during the massacre of Elzawya Elhamra ¶45[39], and the explosion in Tanta's Church ¶54 [39], then **WHAT ELSE THE COURT WOULD ACCEPT TO GIVE HIM STANDING? AND HOW CAN HE RESOLVE HIS GRIEVANCE?** Moreover, the Fatwas (Sharia's decree) to assassinate everyone that criticizes any thing about Islam, are well known against Salman Rushdie, Geert Wilders, Hamed Abdel Samad, etc. We have the followers of Sharia killing tens of thousands of innocent people including women and children in the Middle East, Africa, and Asia, thousands in Europe, and hundreds in the USA, hence, just for Plaintiff to file this complaint is more than enough to **make him a specific target** and **endanger his life**. Plaintiff suffered and lived through Islamic terror

with most of his injuries were outside the USA. However, the <u>Court overlooked</u> that the Islamic State through its followers of Sharia, **declared war against all** that that are not part of the Islamic State including the USA. They are here, and are **coming, to commit their terror** and guerilla warfare. Up until now no one was able to stop them ¶85[39].

3) As for Counts I to VIII, the Court overlooked that there are **specific injuries** to Plaintiff not common to the public in general. Examples are that not everyone has: a) relatives that want to migrate to the USA; b) migrants that their immigration was delayed due to the illegal ones; c) relatives that need asylum; d) suffered from religious discrimination; e) suffered fron Sharia; and/or f) suffered or lived through Islamic terror.

4) The Court overlooked that Counts I to IV are **not addressing immigration laws**, but to protect this country from the terror of Islamic guerilla war. They are to **declare** that Sharia is at war with our Constitution, laws, and country; **ban** its application; and avoid its dangers by **enjoining** those who believe in its violent teachings from entering the USA.

5) The Court overlooked Plaintiff's argument in ¶12[61] for the dissenting opinion that "*[S]tanding is not to be denied simply because many people suffer the same injury*" [United States v. Richardson, 418 U.S. 204 (1974)]. Plaintiff believes that denying standing because he seeks "*relief that would affect him no more directly than the public at large*" is **unconstitutional** and violates the First Amendment.

6) It is an axiomatic principle in law that at this stage of litigation, Plaintiff is not required to prove his injuries; he is required to allege facts to support his claims.

7) The Court did not support Defendants' argument that the **threat** of Islamic war motivated by **Sharia** is abstract or not-plausible, which asserts Plaintiff's injuries asserting his standing. The reality of Islamic terror was demonstrated again on 12/11/2017, when an

Islamic terrorist tried to detonate a bomb in New York. The authorities tried to **pathetically justify their failures** by saying that he was a "Lone **Wolf**", which is **admitting that he is a Wolf,** as if they **want these Wolves to attack in packs**, so that they can stop them. This proves again Plaintiff's arguments about the dangers of Sharia and the failures of our government.

8) Plaintiff was fearing for his safety and the **safety of the Court** if he files this case because any fear could **dramatically affect the Court's decision.** This fear motivated him to ask the authorities and the Court for protection [33]. However, Plaintiff felt that doing an **open public trial** will expose the **grave dangers** of **Sharia, and corruption; negligence; and bias of our government**. Plaintiff avoided the religious arguments focusing mainly on the legal facts, and chose a jury trial to reduce the pressure on the Judge.

9) Plaintiff expected that the **DOJ's lawyers** involved in this case would support what is good for the country and **the citizens** (including Plaintiff as a citizen), but realized that they were **trying to destroy President Trump** (see paragraphs 1, 2, 7, 9, 23 of [61]). Just a few days ago, new facts uncovered **damaging proofs** that **high ranking officials** in the **DOJ** and the FBI were working hard **to destroy President Trump** even if this **will destroy the Country**, which is the same thing the **DOJ**'s lawyers are doing in this case [https://www.reuters.com/article/us-usa-trump-russia/senior-justice-official-dismisses-republican-charges-of-bias-in-trump-probe-idUSKBN1E728J], [http://www.foxnews.com/politics/2017/12/07/top-doj-official-demoted-amid-probe-contacts-with-trump-dossier-firm.html]. Therefore, **Farag as a citizen, not as a plaintiff,** is demanding that these **DOJ's lawyers that proved their bias against the President, must inform the Defendants personally** about the case and **get their approvals** for the strategies to oppose or **support** the complaint.

10) At the beginning of July 2017, Plaintiff started sending different complaints to President Trump, Secretary of State, Attorney General, and Chief of Staff, but did not receive any response up until now. Beginning the last week of November 2017, Plaintiff started submitting claims for the destruction of his nuclear business to: 1) Dept. of Energy; 2) Dept. of Defense; 3) CIA; 4) FBI; 5) Attorney General; 6) Dept. of Homeland Security; 7) Dept. of Interior; 8) Dept. of State; 9) Committee for Foreign Investment (Treasury Dept.); 10) Office of Inspector General; and 11) Dept. of Justice. Plaintiff received a response from Dept. of State informing him that they do not respond to such complaints and they referred it to the Office of Inspector General.

11) Plaintiff discovered that the destruction of our nuclear industry was done by executing a well-orchestrated plan to destroy all and every element of our nuclear industry.

WHEREFORE, Plaintiff Tarek Farag prays that this Honorable Court reconsider its order dismissing his complaint, or in the alternative allow Counts I to IV and grant a writ of certiorari to the Supreme Court to resolve the issue of standing, and grant other relief as just.

Respectfully submitted,

Plaintiff: TAREK FARAG, pro se
Date: December 19, 2017

29. ORDER DENYING PLAINTIFF'S MOTION TO RECONSIDER

NOTIFICATION OF DOCKET ENTRY

This docket entry was made by the Clerk on Wednesday, December 20, 2017:

MINUTE entry before the Honorable Gary Feinerman: Motion to reconsider the Court order dismissing the complaint is [71] is denied. Plaintiff offers no basis to disturb the judgment. Motion hearing set for 1/10/2018 [72] is stricken. Mailed notice.(jlj,)

30. THE NUCLEAR CRIME OF THE CENTURY

THE DESTRUCTION OF ALL THE ELEMENTS OF THE NUCLEAR INDUSTRY OF THE USA

In this section, I will try to explain in a simple way all the elements of the nuclear industry to allow the non-technical person to understand the issues and grasp the size and danger of its destruction. We need to notice that about 20% of the electricity in the USA is coming from nuclear power stations, and nuclear power generation has zero gas emission. We have ignorant politicians making technical decisions, while the technical people are stuck with these decisions and their disastrous concequences.

The main element in the nuclear industry is uranium, which has two main isotopes U238 and U235. In its natural existence, the U235 represents a small percentage of about 0.7%. Nuclear reactors could be designed using natural uranium under restrict conditions, however, modern reactors use uranium with the percentage of U235 increased to levels of 4% to 10%, with a process called enrichment. When a neutron bombards the atom of U235 it can go into fission releasing nuclear energy and generating more than two neutrons. When a neutron bombards the U238 atom it converts it into plutonium. Plutonium is fissionable like the U235, but its reaction to a neutron hitting it, is faster than U235. This is why plutonium is more suitable for weapons than U235 (need to react quickly to increase the power of explosion) and difficult to use in nuclear power reactors (difficult to slow down the reaction to be able to control it).

After the previous simple discussion, we can state the main elements of the nuclear industry, guided by the report of the World

Nuclear Association [http://www.world-nuclear.org/information-library/country-profiles/countries-t-z/usa-nuclear-fuel-cycle.aspx] in the following:
1- Extracting uranium from its ores (mining).
2- Conversion.
3- Enrichment.
4- Deconversion.
5- Fuel fabrication.
6- Building and running nuclear reactors to generate power.
7- Reprocessing the burned (used) uranium.
8- Disposal of the radioactive materials.

1- Uranium mining
The USA ranks ninth in the world for known uranium resources. At peak production, the USA had over 250 operational mines, the mining kept declining until there are only two operational mines. Some of the reasons of mining decline are the restrictions and the banning imposed on uranium mining, which started by previous administrations and reached its peak during Obama's Administration destroying the first element of the nuclear industry.

2- Uranium conversion
Converting uranium oxide, U_3O_8, to uranium hexafluoride UF_6, to use for enrichment process, was done by the Honeywell plant, which is the only conversion plant in the USA. Due to the decline in the demand for the enrichments inside the USA, Honeywell announced in November 2017, that it was idling production at the plant, destroying this element of the nuclear industry.

3- Uranium enrichment
The USA currently has one operating enrichment plant owned by Urenco. It produces less than one third of the domestic demand, instead of producing ten times its capacity to meet the global demand. This represents a huge loss for the USA as a leading country in innovation and technology. Ironically the Obama Administration allowed Iran to build and develop uranium enrichment, while killing ours, which is a destruction of this third element of the nuclear industry.

4- Deconversion

Deconversion of the depleted uranium hexafluoride that remains as a byproduct after enrichment has not so far been undertaken on a large scale in the USA, and is considered a waste that cost money to get rid of. Hence, this forth element of the nuclear industry does not exist (destroyed).

5- Fuel fabrication

Fuel fabrication is the conversion of enriched uranium oxide into solid pellets for fuel rods. It is in some way similar to filling the natural gas into cylinders for home use, which does not require high technical expertise. There are facilities operated by Westinghouse fabricating 1500 t/y, GEH's Global Nuclear Fuel (owned by GE, Hitachi and Toshiba) fabricating 1500 t/y, and other facilities some of them are under construction and others having difficulties in operation and financing. The EIA's Uranium Marketing Annual Report for 2016 said that 22,956 tonnes of U_3O_8 (equivalent) was purchased by US utilities in 2016. The total fabrication capacity of the USA is about 3000 t/y, which is a negligible 13% of the total demand, indicating another destruction of the fabrication element.

6- Building and running nuclear reactors to generate power

The Obama's Administration policy was to kill the generation of electricity by nuclear reactors, although, it has zero gas emission and represents about 20% of the total electricity generated. In spite of the latest technical advancements that can reduce the dangers to humans in operating nuclear reactors, which would allow the updating of the reactors, they are decommissioning them at an average cost of $300 million each. The total amount accumulated for the decommissioning at the end of 2012, was $45.7 billion, which are coming from the unsuspecting consumers. This puts the USA in a disastrous position.

7- Reprocessing the burned (used) uranium

The disastrous policy of the USA was to prevent the reprocessing of reactor fuels. However, there are some trials that face many obstacles for reprocessing. To understand the importance of reprocessing imagine $U235$ as coal in a furnace mixed with $U238$ as an impurities that can generate plutonium as burnable gasses. Once you ignite the burnable gasses, they will burn quickly without any control. While you can control the burning of the coal, in a way to produce burnable toxic gasses in different ratios. If you decide not to burn these gasses by recycling them to the furnace, you have to safely dispose them at very large cost and loss of their energy. This is the same with reactor fuel. During the burning of U235 (coal), it converts U238 (impurities), to burnable toxic plutonium (burnable gasses) plus additional radioactive materials some of which have long life of radioactivity that can last thousands of years. Both plutonium and the radioactive materials need very expensive disposal. The smart choice is to uncontrollably burn the recycled plutonium (burnable gasses) to generate part of the power and generate the rest from the controllable burning of the U235 (coal), and feed in the reactor the long-lived radioactive materials to be burned to elements of shorter life of radioactivity. This way we reuse the plutonium, avoid its toxicity, generate more power, reduce the amount of waste, and the volume and cost of disposing the waste.

8- **Disposal of the radioactive materials**

The policy forbidding the reprocessing of the used fuel, resulted in larger amounts of dangerous waste, which is estimated to be about 2000 t/y (which is still very small compared to the 115 million t/y of ash generated from coal [1/57500]). Obama and his administration went into a spree of attacking the nuclear industry, following the 2009 presidential elections, by policy changes, budget cuts, and aborting projects like the waste disposal project of the Yucca Mountain. Then in August 2013, the federal Appeals Court ordered the NRC to resume its review of DOE's application to license, construct, and operate the Yucca Mountain repository. The court said that the case "raises significant questions about the scope of the Executive's authority to disregard federal statutes". In summary, the nuclear waste disposal is in big mess:
- Some Counties are opposing constructing disposal sites in unjustified fear or radiation, and others requesting them for financial benefits;
- Some waste is stored on site of the reactor, and other transferred to other locations;

- Billions of dollars are spent on studies that eventually go to the drains; etc.

One of the methods to get rid of the highly radioactive materials with long half-life is to burn them in a reactor to convert them to materials with low or no radioactivity.

31. LETTER TO TRUMP WARNING HIM FROM THE RUSSIA CRAZE

CONFIDENTIAL and PERSONAL

RUSSIA, RUSSIA, RUSSIA, THE REAL STORY OF CLINTONS AND OBAMA

July 18, 2017

TO:

DONALD J. TRUMP, PRESIDENT OF THE UNITED STATES
JEFF SESSIONS, U.S. ATTORNEY GENERAL

My name is Tarek Farag, I finished my PhD in Nuclear Engineering 1988, and immediately migrated from Egypt to the USA. On Feb. 2006 applied for a patent to separate uranium isotopes for civilian or military applications at very high speed and low cost. It could save Illinois more than $400 Million per year in electricity cost. Due to its sensitivity to our national security, I sued the government to keep it secret, but failed due to procedural issues, and ended up patenting it in the USA (9,056,272), Canada (2674952), and Australia (2007220850). When trying to apply this patent in the USA, I discovered the disastrous fact that we do not have nuclear industry. Bill Clinton, Hillary Clinton, and Obama sold our Nuclear Industry a long time ago to Russia and then destroyed it for the Russian's benefit and their own personal gain. This is the reason for this craze about Russia, Russia, Russia, to divert the attention away from their crimes and to distract Trump.

The most disturbing thing is that full information about these crimes are available to the public (some references are listed) but no one took any action. The elements of these crimes are:

1. The Obama administration with Clintons (OC) said that they sold small percentage of our Nuclear Industry to Russia but in reality, it was more than 80%.
2. OC banned the mining of uranium in many areas to kill uranium production.
3. OC tried to confiscate uranium-rich lands for Uranium One (eventually to Russia).
4. OC subsidized solar-panels and limited the construction of new nuclear power stations.

These crimes made most of the nuclear companies struggle and some were bankrupt, as shown from today's share prices of the following companies: Energy Fuels, Inc. ($1.78); Peninsula Energy ($0.28); Azarga Uranium ($0.24); Anfield Resources ($0.052).

PLEASE PROSECUTE THESE CRIMES IMMEDIATELY.

Sincerely,

TAREK FARAG

https://www.washingtonpost.com/national/2016/11/01/c45bdf4e-a04c-11e6-a44d-cc2898cfab06_story.html?utm_term=.c5c30105a199
https://www.nytimes.com/2015/04/24/us/cash-flowed-to-clinton-foundation-as-russians-pressed-for-control-of-uranium-company.html
http://www.wnd.com/2016/01/oregon-shootout-rooted-in-clinton-uranium-trade/
https://www.reddit.com/r/WikiLeaks/comments/5gx351/hillary_clinton_uranium_one_and_the_bundy_blm/
http://www.dcclothesline.com/2016/05/21/bundy-ranch-political-prisoner-hillary-clinton-government-land-grabs-uranium/

32. LETTER TO TRUMP WARNING HIM FROM THE DOJ

CONFIDENTIAL and PERSONAL

TRUMP'S GOVERNMENT LAWYERS TRYING TO DESTROY HIM

July 11, 2017

TO:

DONALD J. TRUMP, PRESIDENT OF THE UNITED STATES
1600 Pennsylvania Ave NW, Washington, DC 20500

JEFF SESSIONS, U.S. ATTORNEY GENERAL
950 Pennsylvania Avenue, NW, Washington, DC 20530-0001

In support of our GREAT PRESIDENT, to protect the USA by his Executive Orders, I filed case **17-cv-02307** [Chicago], titled Farag vs. Trump, et al. **This case is based on LEGAL FACTS** about Islamic ideology and **NOT ISLAM AS A RELIGION**, and emphasizes that **Muslims are humans** (like all humans) **that their acts can change according to Islam's teachings.**

Farag claims that Obama's Administration was grossly negligent and could have been complacent in the Islamic terrorists' attacks because they had enough warnings and information to prevent them, but they did not. Farag asks the Court:
1. BAN SHARIA because it is contrary to the Constitution and laws of the U.S.;
2. BAN THE ENTRANCE OF MUSLIMS to the U.S. except those who denounce clearly, explicitly, and honestly, the teachings of Islam that do not comply with our laws, and present their religious books clear from any incompliant, unlawful, or violent teachings;
3. Compel the Defendants to properly vet people entering the U.S.;
4. Compel Defendants to enforce our immigration laws; etc.

Unfortunately, the government lawyers representing our **President** are **not defending him** but trying to **destroy and humiliate him, consistent with what happened in all the cases against Trump's Travel Ban**. Where the **court illegally expanded its jurisdiction and power to issue judgments in favor of unknown plaintiffs, not parties to the case, not U.S. citizens, and in foreign countries**. Not a single government lawyer objected to this or any other illegal actions by these courts, they all should be fired. Those kinds of lawyers are trying to **DISMISS** Farag's case without **examining its MERITS, in violation of their duties and the public trust**. The Court's documents prove it beyond any doubt, and I am ready to email them all to save time.

PLEASE TAKE IMMEDIATE ACTION TO STOP THEM, DRAIN THE SWAMPS, CLEAN THE ADMINISTRATION, AND MAKE AMERICA GREAT AGAIN.

Sincerely,

TAREK FARAG

33. LETTER TO TRUMP WARNING AND INFORMING HIM ABOUT THE COURT CASE TO SUPPORT HIM

CONFIDENTIAL and PERSONAL

WE ELECTED YOU TO MAKE PEACE WITH RUSSIA, ELIMINATE ISIS, AND MAKE PEACE IN SYRIA, NOT TO ATTACK RUSSIA, KILL SYRIAN PEOPLE, AND INVADE AFGHANISTAN
FOLLOW YOUR INSTINCT
WHEN YOU SEE DEMOCRATS HAPPY WITH WHAT YOU DO, KNOW IT IS WRONG
RUSSIA, RUSSIA, RUSSIA, THE REAL STORY OF CLINTONS AND OBAMA

August 31, 2017

TAREK FARAG

TO: DONALD J. TRUMP, PRESIDENT OF THE UNITED STATES
JEFF SESSIONS, U.S. ATTORNEY GENERAL

I filed a very important case **17-cv-02307** [Chicago], titled Farag vs. Trump, et al. **This case is based on LEGAL FACTS** about Islamic ideology and **NOT ISLAM AS A RELIGION**. It is against Trump, but **in reality, it is against Obama**. It is a civil case, but contains many allegations of criminal activities that need criminal prosecution. I am asking the Court:

1. Declare that **SHARIA IS INCOMPATIBLE AND CONTRARY** to the Constitution and laws of the United States, and **SHOULD BE BANNED**;
2. **Enjoin the application of Sharia** in all the USA;
3. Enjoin the people that believe in Sharia from entering the USA;
4. Issue an order **ENJOINING THE ENTRANCE OF MUSLIMS TO THE U.S. except those peaceful ones** who denounce clearly and explicitly without deception, the

teachings of Islam that do not comply with our Constitution or laws, and present their religious references clean from any incompliant, unlawful, or violent teachings;
5. Compel President Donald **Trump to reissue his executive order to ban Muslims** not people from certain countries;
6. Compel the Defendants to **enforce our immigration laws**;
7. Compel the Defendants to vet the people entering the USA to make sure that they do not endanger our wellbeing;
8. **Enjoin** Defendants from admitting **Elsisi** (President of Egypt) or any other foreign government official that **committed violations of freedom of religion** into the USA;
9. Compensate Plaintiff at least $1,800,000,000.00 for destroying his business by the Russian-Uranium deal that destroyed our nuclear industry;
10. Compensate the Plaintiff and his family for their damages; and
11. **Nullify all the actions of Obama and his administration that were biased to Islam**.

Unfortunately, THE GOVERNMENT LAWYERS representing our **President** are **not defending him** but trying to **destroy and humiliate him**. Those kinds of lawyers are trying to **DISMISS** Farag's case without **examining its MERITS, in violation of their duties and the public trust**. The Court's documents prove it beyond any doubt, and I am ready to email them all to save time. **PLEASE TAKE IMMEDIATE ACTION TO STOP AND REPLACE THOSE BAD LAWYERS, DRAIN THE SWAMPS, CLEAN THE ADMINISTRATION, AND MAKE AMERICA GREAT AGAIN.**

Sincerely,

TAREK FARAG

34. LETTER TO TRUMP WARNING AND INFORMING HIM ABOUT THE DESTRUCTION OF OUR NUCLEAR INDUSTRY

My name is Tarek Farag, I finished my PhD in Nuclear Engineering 1988, and immediately migrated from Egypt to the USA. On Feb. 2006 applied for a patent to separate uranium isotopes for civilian or military applications at very high speed and low cost. Due to its sensitivity to our national security, I sued the government to keep it secret, but failed due to procedural issues, and ended up patenting it in the USA (9,056,272), Canada (2674952), and Australia (2007220850). When trying to apply this patent in the USA, I discovered the disastrous fact that we lost our nuclear industry. Bill Clinton, Hillary Clinton, and Obama sold our Nuclear Industry a long time ago to Russia and then destroyed it for the Russian's benefit and their own personal gain. This is the reason for this craze about Russia, Russia, Russia, to divert the attention away from their crimes and to distract Trump.

The most disturbing thing is that full information about these crimes are available to the public (some references are listed) but no one took any action. The elements of these crimes are:
1. The Obama administration with Clintons (OC) said that they sold small percentage of our Nuclear Industry to Russia but in reality, it was more than 90%.
2. OC banned the mining of uranium in many areas to kill uranium production.
3. OC tried to confiscate uranium-rich lands for Uranium One (eventually to Russia).
4. OC subsidized solar-panels and limited the construction of new nuclear power stations.

These crimes made most of the nuclear companies struggle and some were bankrupt, as shown from today's share prices of the following companies: Energy Fuels, Inc. ($1.78); Peninsula Energy ($0.28); Azarga Uranium ($0.24); Anfield Resources ($0.052).

PLEASE PROSECUTE THESE CRIMES IMMEDIATELY.

Sincerely,

TAREK FARAG

https://www.washingtonpost.com/national/2016/11/01/c45bdf4e-a04c-11e6-a44d-cc2898cfab06_story.html?utm_term=.c5c30105a199
https://www.nytimes.com/2015/04/24/us/cash-flowed-to-clinton-foundation-as-russians-pressed-for-control-of-uranium-company.html
http://www.wnd.com/2016/01/oregon-shootout-rooted-in-clinton-uranium-trade/
https://www.reddit.com/r/WikiLeaks/comments/5gx351/hillary_clinton_uranium_one_and_the_bundy_blm/
http://www.dcclothesline.com/2016/05/21/bundy-ranch-political-prisoner-hillary-clinton-government-land-grabs-uranium/

35. GOVERNMENT SUPPORT TO ISLAMIC TERRORISTS

While I was writing this book, many facts became known that proved the hard to believe allegations of our government's intentional support of Islamic terror. One of which is the following article by the great organization **Judicial Watch**.

As FBI Director Mueller Helped Cover Up Fla. 9/11 Probe, Court Docs Show
[https://www.myjw.org/wta/link.php?AGENCY=jw&M=3405686&N=10416&L=5622&F=H]

JANUARY 24, 2018

Court documents recently filed by the government further rock the credibility of Russia Special Counsel Robert Mueller because they show that as FBI Director Mueller he worked to cover up the connection between a Florida Saudi family and the 9/11 terrorist attacks. The documents reveal that Mueller was likely involved in publicly releasing deceptive official agency statements about a secret investigation of the Saudis, who lived in Sarasota, with ties to the hijackers. A Florida journalism nonprofit uncovered [https://www.myjw.org/wta/link.php?AGENCY=jw&M=3405686&N=10416&L=5623&F=H] the existence of the secret FBI investigation that was also kept from Congress.

Under Mueller's leadership, the FBI tried to discredit the story, publicly countering that agents found no connection between the Sarasota Saudi family and the 2001 terrorist plot. The reality is that the FBI's own files contained several reports that said the opposite, according to the Ft. Lauderdale-based news group's ongoing investigation [https://www.myjw.org/wta/link.php?AGENCY=jw&M=3405686&N=10416&L=5624&F=H]. Files obtained by reporters in the course of their lengthy probe reveal that federal agents found "many connections" between the family and "individuals associated with the terrorist attacks on 9/11/2001." The FBI was forced to release the once-secret reports because the news group sued in federal court when the information wasn't provided under the Freedom of Information Act (FOIA).

The disingenuous statements were issued by FBI officials in Miami and Tampa in a desperate effort to disparage a 2011 story exposing the agency's covert investigation of the Sarasota Saudis as well as reporting that it had been concealed from Congress. Mueller is referenced in a document index that was ordered by a federal judge to be created in late November 2017. The south Florida judge, William J. Zloch, a Ronald Reagan appointee, asked the FBI to explain where it had discovered dozens of pages of documents in the public-records case filed six years ago. The index reference to then-FBI Director Mueller appears in an item involving an agency white paper written a week after the publication of a news story about the abrupt departure of Saudis Abdulaziz and Anoud al-Hijji from their Sarasota area home about two weeks before 9/11. The couple left behind their cars, clothes, furniture, jewelry and other personal items. "It was created to brief the FBI Director concerning the FBI's investigation of 4224 Escondito Circle," the al-Hijjis' address, the index says.

Though the recently filed court documents reveal Mueller received a briefing about the Sarasota Saudi investigation, the FBI continued to publicly deny it existed and it appears that the lies were approved by Mueller. Not surprisingly, he didn't respond to questions about this new discovery emailed to his office by the news organization that uncovered it. Though the mainstream media has neglected to report this relevant development, it's difficult to ignore that it chips away at Mueller's credibility as special counsel to investigate if Russia influenced the 2016 presidential election. Even before the Saudi coverup documents were exposed by nonprofit journalists, Mueller's credentials were questionable to head any probe. Back in May Judicial Watch reminded of Mueller's misguided handiwork [https://www.myjw.org/wta/link.php?AGENCY=jw&M=3405686&N=10416&L=5625&F=H] and collaboration with radical Islamist organizations as FBI director.

148

Back in 2013 Judicial Watch exclusively obtained droves of records documenting how, under Mueller's leadership, the FBI purged all anti-terrorism training material deemed "offensive" to Muslims after secret meetings between Islamic organizations and the then-FBI chief. Judicial Watch had to sue [https://www.myjw.org/wta/link.php?AGENCY=jw&M=3405686&N=10416&L=5626&F=H] to get the records and published an in-depth report [https://www.myjw.org/wta/link.php?AGENCY=jw&M=3405686&N=10416&L=5628&F=H] on the scandal in 2013 and a lengthier, updated follow-up in 2015 [https://www.myjw.org/wta/link.php?AGENCY=jw&M=3405686&N=10416&L=5428&F=H]. As FBI director, Mueller bent over backwards to please radical Islamist groups and caved into their demands. The agency eliminated the valuable anti-terrorism training material and curricula after Mueller met with various Islamist organizations, including those with documented ties too terrorism. Among them were two organizations— Islamic Society of North America (ISNA) and Council on American Islamic Relations (CAIR)—named by the U.S. government as unindicted co-conspirators in the 2007 Holy Land Foundation terrorist financing case. CAIR is a terrorist front group with extensive links to foreign and domestic Islamists. It was founded in 1994 by three Middle Eastern extremists (Omar Ahmad, Nihad Awad and Rafeeq Jaber) who ran the American propaganda wing of Hamas, known then as the Islamic Association for Palestine.

36. MASSACRE OF PARKLAND SCHOOL SHOOTING

This time, the intentional negligence of some people in the FBI, the Police, and other Agencies, is very clear and undisputed. I expected this and other terror attacks to happen, they happened, and will continue to happen, until those responsible about stopping these attacks are prosecuted. However, instead of directing the attention to the real reasons and the responsible people, some people are twisting the facts to blame Trump, guns, or the police officers. Luckily, there are many good people like Max Eden (Manhattan Institute) https://www.city-journal.org/html/how-did-parkland-shooter-slip-through-cracks-15741.html, and Bill Marshall (Senior Investigator in Judicial Watch) https://www.judicialwatch.org/video-update/inside-judicial-watch-law-enforcements-failures-parkland-school-shooting/?utm_source=deployer&utm_medium=email&utm_campaign=action+alert&utm_term=members&utm_content=20180307180845, that did a good analysis to the reasons of the miserable failure to stop this massacre. Both concluded that Obama and his administration are the ones responsible about it. I concluded this long ago, and called for their prosecutions. The mentality of purging Muslims from the watch list of Islamic terrorists that lead to many massacres, is the same in keeping the violent students out of police reach because about 70% of them are Blacks and Latinos, which allowed this violent student to execute his massacre under the watch of the Police, FBI, etc.

I will draw the attention to some points.
1. The FBI and the Police had enough warnings and information about the intentions, the determinations, and the preparations to execute the massacre, and no one did anything to prevent it.
2. An officer was inside the school at the start of the shooting, and three officers joined him later, but no one tried to stop the shooter. I believe that the first officer was under pressure to fake a story (many days later) that he thought that the shooter is outside the building. I do not believe it, especially for a police officer.

3. The police prevented the emergency medical help from entering the place to provide immediate treatments to the injured.
4. Instead of calling for the prosecution of the negligent people that allowed this massacre, the Polistitutes and the Medistitute orchestrated demonstrations to blame Trump, Gums, NRA, the Police officer (escape goat), Russia, Russian meddling in the elections, etc. In addition, as always, claiming that the security agencies do not have enough spying power on people.

This massacre brings to my mind serious questions about the **Agencies** that its main function is to prevent such massacre:
    a. **Did they allow it to happen to PROVE that mass killings and terror are NOT LIMITED TO ISLAMIC TERROR?**
    b. Did they allow it to happen to **blame Trump**?
    c. Did they allow it to happen to ask the Congress to give them more power to **spy on people** and **invade their privacy**?
    d. Did they allow it to happen to get the guns out from the hands of good citizens?
    e. Was the circus of Announcement of Indictments of Russians (2 days after the massacre) to distract people?
    f. Did they orchestrate these demonstrations around the country to blame Trump? Where these demonstrators were during the **Islamic** massacres of "Boston Marathon", "San Bernardino", and "Orlando Florida"? Are people in the USA, like people in Europe, **not allowed to protest against Islamic terror**?

37. ROD ROSENSTEIN ANNOUNCED INDICTMENTS OF RUSSIANS IN U.S. ELECTION MEDDLING

https://drive.google.com/file/d/16APDftrAuKM--B1nlk_3LzHhYWmxCHUz/view

I previously stated many times that if the Russians or other foreigners were able to meddle in our elections, it is **our failures not their successes**. I expected this indictment, knowing the extent of the corruption in the DOJ, but never expected it to be at this low level. I thought that this indictment was an Egyptian indictment against the political opponents of the Egyptian president, but later discovered that the corruption of our DOJ surpassed that of the Egyptian government. Not knowing what to do; **should I laugh or cry**, a joke jumped to my mind about the election meddling.

The joke says that Obama was impressed with the way the president of Egypt always gets more than 99% of the votes, and he wanted to get the same results. Obama asked the Egyptian president Mobarak to send some of his top experts to assist him in the American elections. Mobarak sent his best experts to the USA as Obama wanted, and they started their work quickly. Finally, immediately after the closing of the voting places, the U.S. Election Committee sent a fax congratulating Mobarak that he swept the American elections with 99.8% of the votes.

Since I do not trust our Medistitute, I read the news about it from foreign media and downloaded the full text of the court paper. Reading this indictment was one of the most boring readings I made. I do not defend the Russian, or accuse them of wrongdoing without proofs. **Simply, the DOJ in this indictment is ACCUSING those Russian people of SAYING THE TRUTH, and doing their RESEARCH and WORK in the BEST PROFESSIONAL MANNERS**. The best way to show the real nature of the accusations is to state some of the statements as they are in the indictment and comment on them (between square brackets [ ]) or just highlight the awkward words as in the following:

1. They **employed** hundreds of individuals for its online operations, ranging from **creators of fictitious personas** to technical and administrative support. [Since when employing people or hiring technical and administrative people are crimes? Most of us have fictitious names on the internet.]
2. Their organization was **headed by a management** group and **organized into departments**, including: a graphics department; a data analysis department; a search-engine optimization ("SEO") department; an information-technology ("IT") department to maintain the digital infrastructure used in the organization's operations; and a finance department to budget and allocate funding.
3. They **studied the U.S**. population and conducted operations on social media platforms such as YouTube, Facebook, Instagram, and Twitter.
4. They **stated goal** of "spread[ing] distrust towards the candidates and the political system in general."
5. Many other persons worked for the ORGANIZATION.
6. They **tracked and studied groups** on U.S. social media sites - - tracked certain **metrics** like the group's size, the frequency of content placed by the group, and the level of audience engagement with that content, such as the average number of comments or responses to a post.
7. They **purchased equipment** (such as cameras, SIM cards, and drop phones).
8. They **traveled** in and around the United States - - exchanged an intelligence report regarding the trip.
9. **Circulated lists of U.S. holidays** so that specialists could develop and post appropriate account activity.
10. **Wrote about topics** germane to the United States such as U.S. foreign policy and U.S. economic issues, and addressed a range of issues.
11. **Evaluated** the content posted by **specialists** - - Specialists received feedback and directions **to improve the quality** of their posts. - - issued or received guidance on: ratios of text, graphics, and video to use in posts; the number of accounts to operate; and the role of each account.
12. **They were successful** and the size of many organization-controlled groups had **grown to hundreds of thousands** of online followers.

13. They **used** the U.S. **Computer Infrastructure**. And walked in U.S. streets, ate American food, spoke English, etc.
14. They asked **real U.S. citizens** to help organize the rallies and offered money to some of them to help cover the expenses for the rallies. In once case, they found a volunteer to provide signs for a "March for Trump" rally in New York.
15. Used false U.S. personas to <u>organize and coordinate U.S. political rallies in support of then president-elect Trump</u>, while simultaneously using other false U.S. personas to <u>organize and coordinate U.S. political rallies protesting the results of the 2016</u> U.S. presidential election. **If this is true**, it means that those participating in these rallies are corrupt (should be prosecuted). [What is the meaning of a false U.S. persona? After making strange accusations, they wonder "if this is true"!].
16. Deleted and destroyed data, including emails, social media accounts, and other evidence of their activities. [These are private things and no one has the right to ask them about it. What about the government materials that Hillary destroyed?]
17. On or about September 13, 2017, KAVERZINA wrote in an email to a family member: *"We had a slight crisis here at work: the FBI busted our activity (not a joke). So, I got preoccupied with covering tracks together with the colleagues."* [An eight years child would not believe or even repeat this statement, only some people in the DOJ.]
18. Created and purchased Facebook advertisements for their "March for Trump" rally.
19. Used allforusa@yahoo.com, the email address of a false U.S. persona, to send out press releases for the "March for Trump" rally to New York media outlets.
20. Contacted a **real U.S. person** to serve as a recruiter for the "March for Trump" rally.
21. **Purchased advertisements** on Facebook to promote the "Support Hillary. Save American Muslims" rally.
22. **Ordered posters** for the "Support Hillary. Save American Muslims" rally.
23. **Communicated with a real U.S. perso**n about the posters they had ordered for the "Support Hillary. Save American Muslims" rally.
24. Created and purchased Facebook advertisements for the "Down With Hillary" rally in New York.

25. Sent out press releases to over thirty media outlets promoting the "Down With Hillary" rally at Trump Tower in New York City. [In the previous points they accuse them of supporting Trump and attacking Hillary, and on the same time supporting Hillary and attacking Trump, i.e. they are neutral trying to measure the real response of the public.]

26. They spread the following [true] statements:
   1. "You know, a great number of black people support us saying that #HillaryClintonIsNotMyPresident;"
   2. "JOIN our #HillaryClintonForPrison2016;"
   3. "Donald wants to defeat terrorism...Hillary wants to sponsor it;"
   4. "Trump is our only hope for a better future;"
   5. "Ohio Wants Hillary 4 Prison"
   6. "We cannot trust Hillary to take care of our veterans!"
   7. "Hillary is a Satan, and her crimes and lies had proved just how evil she is."

I think that these samples are more than enough to show the kind of this indictment, and those who want to get more should read the entire indictment.

My conclusion from this indictment is that; all who participated in it including Muller and Sessions, should be fired and prosecuted for wasting our resources.

38. WHO POISONED SERGEI SKRIPAL?

I start by stating my own conclusion that he was poisoned (if he was really poisoned) by the Western Intelligence Agencies, especially the British and the U.S. I do not have my own resources or connections to people that know secret information; hence, this conclusion is based on my own analysis using the publicly available and not trustworthy information on the Internet and other media.

My first set of reasons to conclude that the Russians are not behind this poisoning is that:
- He was a Russian double-agent, convicted and imprisoned in 2006 for passing the identities of Russian agents working undercover in Europe to the **British Foreign Intelligence Service**.
- Russia freed him in 2010 as part of a **U.S.-Russian spy swap** and he moved to Britain.
- After being in jail for four years, he lost his value as a spy and did not represent any threat to the Russians, especially after they discovered his spying activities.
- If the Russians were interested in assassinating him, they could have done it very easily without any penalties.
- Hence, Russia has no interest or motive to poison him.

My other sets of reasons to conclude that Russia is not behind this poisoning, which **could be orchestrated** by the **British and the U.S. intelligence agencies**, especially with nerve gas, are that:
- They have a **history of obsession of falsely accusing Russia and its allies with using nerve gas without any proof**. For example: accusing countries of gassing their own people. Iraq, Serbia, Libya, Syria, ad nauseam.
- They can **hide their false evidence** from the world and the Russians, claiming that they cannot disclose them because they involve top-secret intelligence methods; hence, they can keep everyone in the dark and reject any request from Russia to examine the investigations.
- This spy is the best target they can use and sacrifice to deceive the idiots and make them believe that the Russians

are trying to show that they can reach their enemies at any place and time.
- They failed miserably (could be intentionally) in performing their main function of protecting their countries from their main enemy "Islamic terror". To **keep their jobs and power**, they invented this Russian monster that controls every thing in their countries from meddling in their politics to walking in their streets and eating their food.
- They are trying to make Russia the big enemy to divert the attention away from their support to the clearly visible Islamic terror.
- They believe in their sacred right to do things that other countries cannot do.
- It is a part of the anti-Trump movement to destroy Trump and his efforts to fulfill his promise to cooperate with the Russians and improve its relationship with the U.S. Including Muller's Russian-Investigations.
- Feed this crazy Nikki Haley with something to continue her screams to destroy our international policies.

We need to notice that, mainly the CIA with other intelligence agencies previously determined the foreign policies of the U.S. The president had little to do against the fake reports and information that they provided him; he could not challenge any of them or would be accused of treason. The Infamous CIA officer E. Howard Hunt disclosed that the CIA was behind the JFK assassination [https://www.maryferrell.org/pages/The_CIA_and_the_JFK_Assassination.html]. Which ascertain the continuations of the same trends of the CIA; of faking reports and inventing enemies to control the policies, while hiding behind the secrecy, hoping that no one would discover the truth.

Later developments in the case of the poisoning of Skripal and his daughter are proving my conclusion that the whole case against Russia is a big lie orchestrated and spread by the British and other non-Russian intelligence agencies. However, what worries me the most is the collapse of the Free-World values and justice system. We have the prime minister of Britain say that Russia is **highly likely** the one who committed this crime, issue a judgment against it, and then execute the judgment by punishing Russia. All that, without allowing the Russian or any neutral party to examine any of the evidence, or do the normal procedures according to the international agreements or standards. We need to notice that in the cases of using poisonous gases, the OPCW (Organization for the Prohibition of Chemical Weapons) should be informed, blood samples of the victims should be collected, and other procedures must be followed. Nevertheless, the British authorities refused to involve the OPCW to avoid exposing their lies. Previously, as there were continuous wars among the intelligence agencies of countries, in the situation when a country cannot present the evidence (for any reason) it would keep silent, or as the saying: "Show the evidence! Shit or get off the pot".

APPENDIX

Exhibit 0

LIST OF EXHIBITS

0- **Exhibit 0**: List of exhibits, which is this exhibit.

1- **Exhibit 1**: The book "Can Trump Defeat Hillary, Obama, Islamic Terror, Prostituted Media, And Political Prostitution", By "AboElhak ElHakani", 7 th. Edition, October 2016. It has an academic study of Islam.

2- **Exhibit 2**: The full Arabic text of the Quran "قرآن كريم" as authorized by AlAzhar (The oldest and most-respected authority by Muslims for the Islamic teachings) as published many centuries ago. Muslims consider it coming from Allah to humans, its text is a holy linguistic miracle, very precise, valid for all societies and all times, no one should dare to change a single letter in it. It is the main source of the Islamic **Sharia** Law. Although Muslims refuse to translate it to encourage the spread of Islam and the Arabic language, there are inaccurate English translations that represent a "Cute" version of Quran.

3- **Exhibit 3**: The most popular and respected book about Sharia in Arabic language, which is studied in Islamic secondary schools in Egypt and other countries. It was published hundreds of years ago, but still the main authority in Sharia. Its Arabic title is: " الإقناع في حل ألفاظ أبي شجاع ". It consist of 3 volumes:

3a- **Exhibit 3a**: Sharia study course for first year in Islamic secondary schools.

3b- **Exhibit 3b**: Sharia study course for second year in Islamic secondary schools.

3c- **Exhibit 3c**: Sharia study course for third year in Islamic secondary schools.

4- **Exhibit 4**: Judicial Watch: Homeland Security Records Reveal Officials Ordered Terrorist Watch List Scrubbed.

5- **Exhibit 5**: Obama Admin Refuses to Inform Congress of 'Islamic Terrorism' in U.S. Officials ignore congressional call to testify about radicalism.

6- **Exhibit 6**: DHS ordered me to scrub records of Muslims with terror ties.

7- **Exhibit 7**: DOJ: Social Media Posts Trashing Muslims May Violate Civil Rights.

8- **Exhibit 8**: Hillary Clinton Welcomes Banned Islamic Radicals.

9- **Exhibit 9**: Could You Be A Criminal? US Supports UN Anti-Free Speech Measure.

> **Note**: To refer to exhibits, the expression "Please refer to Exhibit 3c page 23" is stated as [E3cp23], and "see Exhibit 2" as [E2].

THE INTERNET LOCATIONS OF THE EXHIBITS IN LIST 0

1- **Exhibit 1**: The book "Can Trump Defeat Hillary, Obama, Islamic Terror, Prostituted Media, And Political Prostitution", By "AboElhak ElHakani", 7 th. Edition, October 2016.
It has an academic study of Islam, analysis to Obama's actions, exposes the Polistitutes and the Medistitute, and analysis of the opposition to Trump during the elections.
https://www.amazon.com/Hillary-Islamic-Prostituted-Political-Prostitutes/dp/1537225790

2- **Exhibit 2**: The full Arabic text of the Quran "قرآن كريم" as authorized by AlAzhar (The oldest and most-respected authority by Muslims for the Islamic teachings) as published many centuries ago. Muslims consider it coming from Allah to humans, its text is a holy linguistic miracle, very precise, valid for all societies and all times, no one should dare to change a single letter in it. It is the main source of the Islamic **Sharia** Law. Although Muslims refuse to translate it to encourage the spread of Islam and the Arabic language, there are inaccurate English translations that represent a "Cute" version of Quran.
http://www.mediafire.com/file/z5c4vapge1j70em/%D8%A7%D9%84%D9%82%D8%B1%D8%A2%D9%86+%D8%A7%D9%84%D9%83%D8%B1%D9%8A%D9%85+%D9%83%D8%A7%D9%85%D9%84%D8%A7.doc

3- **Exhibit 3**: The most popular and respected book about Sharia in Arabic language, which is studied in Islamic secondary schools in Egypt and other countries. It was published hundreds of years ago, but still the main authority in Sharia. Its Arabic title is:
"الإقناع في حل ألفاظ أبي شجاع", published 2010. It consist of 3 volumes:
   3a- **Exhibit 3a**: Sharia study course for first year in Islamic secondary schools.
   http://www.shamela.ws/index.php/book/6121

   3b- **Exhibit 3b**: Sharia study course for second year in Islamic secondary schools.

http://www.shamela.ws/index.php/book/6121

3c- **Exhibit 3c**: Sharia study course for third year in Islamic secondary schools.
http://www.shamela.ws/index.php/book/6121

4- **Exhibit 4**: Judicial Watch: Homeland Security Records Reveal Officials Ordered Terrorist Watch List Scrubbed**.**
https://www.judicialwatch.org/press-room/press-releases/judicial-watch-homeland-security-records-reveal-officials-ordered-terrorist-watch-list-scrubbed/

5- **Exhibit 5**: Obama Admin Refuses to Inform Congress of 'Islamic Terrorism' in U.S. Officials ignore congressional call to testify about radicalism**.** **http://freebeacon.com/national-security/obama-admin-refuses-inform-congress-islamic-terrorism-u-s/**

6- **Exhibit 6**: DHS ordered me to scrub records of Muslims with terror ties**.** **http://thehill.com/blogs/congress-blog/homeland-security/268282-dhs-ordered-me-to-scrub-records-of-muslims-with-terror**

7- **Exhibit 7**: DOJ: Social Media Posts Trashing Muslims May Violate Civil Rights.
https://www.judicialwatch.org/blog/2013/05/doj-social-media-posts-trashing-muslims-may-violate-civil-rights/

8- **Exhibit 8**: Hillary Clinton Welcomes Banned Islamic Radicals**.**
https://www.judicialwatch.org/blog/2010/01/clinton-welcomes-banned-islamic-radicals/

9- **Exhibit 9**: Could You Be A Criminal? US Supports UN Anti-Free Speech Measure**.**
https://www.forbes.com/sites/abigailesman/2011/12/30/could-you-be-a-criminal-us-supports-un-anti-free-speech-measure/#588de1c33560

Exhibit 10

SECOND LIST OF EXHIBITS

0- **Exhibit 10**: Second list of exhibits, which is this exhibit.
1- **Exhibit 11**: The New York Times article on April 23, 2015, showing the cash flowing to Clinton Foundation amid Russian Uranium Deal (Exh11ClintonRussianUDeal.pdf).
2- **Exhibit 12**: The history of donations to the Clinton Foundation, and the Russian Uranium Takeover. (Exh12Donations2Clinton4RussiaUDeal.pdf)
3- **Exhibit 13**: U.S. Energy Information Administration [EIA] Uranium purchased by owners and operators of U.S. civilian nuclear power reactors, 1994-2016. Showing the domestic supply of Uranium to USA nuclear reactors was 16.6% on 2013, 6.2% on 2014, and 6.02% on 2015 (Exh13UFromUSA4Elect.pdf).
4- **Exhibit 14**: Investigation ties Hillary's Russian deal to Rancher-Fed standoff. (Exh14OregonShootoutClintonUDeal.pdf).
5- **Exhibit 15**: WikiLeaks: Hillary Clinton and pay for play criminal activity with the Uranium One deal (Exh15HillaryU1BundyProtestWikiLeaks.pdf).
6- **Exhibit 16**: Pete Santilli claims there is circumstantial evidence that Hillary Clinton is involved in the using of the Bureau of Land Management to grab Uranium mines to Russia (Exh16BundyRanchHillaryLandGrabUranium .pdf).
7- **Exhibit 17**: Hawaii's Court order granting motion for Temporary Restraining Order (Exh17HawiiTrmpOrdrTRO.pdf).
8- **Exhibit 18**: Order of 9th Circuit against government's emergency motion (Exh18ApplOrder9thCirTrump.pdf).
9- **Exhibit 19**: Supreme Court enforces Trump's executive order. (Exh19SupSrtEnforceBan.pdf)
10- **Exhibit 20:** Order of 9th Circuit of Appeal against government's EO2.
11- **Exhibit 21:** Uranium marketing report released June 19,2017.
12- **Exhibit 22:** Farag's Patent No. 9,056,272, for Isotope Separation and Purification.
13- **Exhibit 23:** Some pages from the book "Islamic Fascism" by Hamed Abdel Samad.

THE INTERNET LOCATIONS OF THE EXHIBITS IN LIST 10

1- **Exhibit 11**: The New York Times article on April 23, 2015, showing the cash flowing to Clinton Foundation amid Russian Uranium Deal (Exh11ClintonRussianUDeal.pdf).
https://www.nytimes.com/2015/04/24/us/cash-flowed-to-clinton-foundation-as-russians-pressed-for-control-of-uranium-company.html

2- **Exhibit 12**: The history of donations to the Clinton Foundation, and the Russian Uranium Takeover. (Exh12Donations2Clinton4RussiaUDeal.pdf)
https://www.nytimes.com/interactive/2015/04/23/us/clinton-foundation-donations-uranium-investors.html

3- **Exhibit 13**: U.S. Energy Information Administration [EIA] Uranium purchased by owners and operators of U.S. civilian nuclear power reactors, 1994-2016. Showing the domestic supply of Uranium to USA nuclear reactors was 16.6% on 2013, 6.2% on 2014, and 6.02% on 2015 (Exh13UFromUSA4Elect.pdf).
https://www.eia.gov/uranium/marketing/html/summarytable1a.php

4- **Exhibit 14**: Investigation ties Hillary's Russian deal to Rancher-Fed standoff. (Exh14OregonShootoutClintonUDeal.pdf).
http://www.wnd.com/2016/01/oregon-shootout-rooted-in-clinton-uranium-trade/

5- **Exhibit 15**: WikiLeaks: Hillary Clinton and pay for play criminal activity with the Uranium One deal (Exh15HillaryU1BundyProtestWikiLeaks.pdf).
https://www.reddit.com/r/WikiLeaks/comments/5gx351/hillary_clinton_uranium_one_and_the_bundy_blm/

6- **Exhibit 16**: Pete Santilli claims there is circumstantial evidence that Hillary Clinton is involved in the using of the Bureau of Land Management to grab Uranium mines to Russia (Exh16BundyRanchHillaryLandGrabUranium .pdf).
http://www.dcclothesline.com/2016/05/21/bundy-ranch-political-

prisoner-hillary-clinton-government-land-grabs-uranium/

7- **Exhibit 17**: Hawaii's Court order granting motion for Temporary Restraining Order (Exh17HawaiiTrmpOrdrTRO.pdf).
https://www.buffalo.edu/content/dam/www/immigration-update/AILA%20-%20Hawaii%20v.%20Trump,%20CV%2017-00050%20DKW-KSC%20-%20Order%20Granting%20Motion%20for%20TRO%2020170315.pdf

8- **Exhibit 18**: Order of 9th Circuit against government's emergency motion (Exh18ApplOrder9thCirTrump.pdf).
https://cdn.ca9.uscourts.gov/datastore/opinions/2017/02/09/17-35105.pdf

9- **Exhibit 19**: Supreme Court enforces Trump's executive order. (Exh19SupSrtEnforceBan.pdf)
https://www.aclu.org/legal-document/international-refugee-assistance-project-v-trump-supreme-court-order-cert-petition

10- **Exhibit 20:** Order of 9th Circuit of Appeal against government's EO2.
https://cdn.ca9.uscourts.gov/datastore/opinions/2017/06/12/17-15589.pdf

11- **Exhibit 21:** Uranium marketing report released June 19, 2017.
https://www.eia.gov/uranium/marketing/

12- **Exhibit 22:** Farag's Patent No. 9,056,272, for Isotope Separation and Purification.
http://patft.uspto.gov/netacgi/nph-Parser?Sect1=PTO1&Sect2=HITOFF&d=PALL&p=1&u=%2Fnetahtml%2FPTO%2Fsrchnum.htm&r=1&f=G&l=50&s1=9,056,272.PN.&OS=PN/9,056,272&RS=PN/9,056,272

13- **Exhibit 23:** Some pages from the book "Islamic Fascism" by Hamed Abdel Samad.
https://www.amazon.com/Islamic-Fascism-Hamed-Abdel-Samad/dp/1633881245

www.ingramcontent.com/pod-product-compliance
Lightning Source LLC
Chambersburg PA
CBHW071542220526
45469CB00003B/893